Unmarried Parents' Rights (and Responsibilities)

3rd Edition

Jacqueline D. Stanley
Attorney at Law

SPHINX® PUBLISHING
AN IMPRINT OF SOURCEBOOKS, INC.®
NAPERVILLE, ILLINOIS
www.SphinxLegal.com

Third Edition: 2005

Published by: **Sphinx® Publishing, An Imprint of Sourcebooks, Inc.®**

Naperville Office
P.O. Box 4410
Naperville, Illinois 60567-4410
630-961-3900
Fax: 630-961-2168
www.sourcebooks.com
www.SphinxLegal.com

This publication is designed to provide accurate and authoritative information in
regard to the subject matter covered. It is sold with the understanding that the publisher is not engaged in rendering legal, accounting, or other professional service. If
legal advice or other expert assistance is required, the services of a competent professional person should be sought.
*From a Declaration of Principles Jointly Adopted by a Committee of the
American Bar Association and a Committee of Publishers and Associations*

This product is not a substitute for legal advice.
Disclaimer required by Texas statutes.

Library of Congress Cataloging-in-Publication Data
Stanley, Jacqueline D.
  Unmarried parents' rights (and Responsibilities) / Jacqueline D. Stanley.-- 3rd ed.
    p. cm.
  Includes index.
  ISBN-13: 978-1-57248-530-3
  ISBN-10: 1-57248-530-2 (alk. paper)
  1. Single parents--Legal status, laws, etc.--United States--Popular works.
  2. Parent and child (Law)--United States--Popular works. I. Title.

KF547.Z9S73 2005
346.7301'7--dc22
                                                                            2005014538

Printed and bound in the United States of America.
BG — 10 9 8 7 6 5 4 3 2 1

CONTENTS

Child Support Law and Procedure
Evaluating Your Situation
Preparing and Filing Legal Forms
Notifying Necessary Parties
The Hearing

Termination of Parental Rights Law and Procedure
Preparing and Filing Legal Forms
Notifying Necessary Parties
The Hearing

INTRODUCTION

This book is designed to be a practical, *how to* guide for people who have children born out of wedlock. It will help you to understand and protect your legal rights, whether you decide to act on your own or through a lawyer.

Although this book is not specifically designed for divorced parents, most of the legal concepts relating to child custody, visitation, and support will also apply to divorced parents. Stepparents are in a unique class and their rights are beyond the scope of this book.

I have dispensed with as much legal jargon and legal theory as possible. There will be no discussion of what the law should be. This book is a practical guide to what the law is and how the system works.

PARENTAL RIGHTS

There are two basic sources of parental rights:
1. the United States Constitution and
2. the laws of the individual states.

Each of these sources are supplemented by decisions of federal and state courts.

In general, as long as there is no abuse or neglect, the government cannot interfere with how we raise our children. Further, the U.S. Constitution sets forth principles of individual freedom, which have been interpreted to give parents a right to a certain degree of privacy with their children. Within these Constitutional limits, each state has the authority to develop laws and procedures that pertain to the relationship between a parent and child. For example, each state may determine how paternity can be established; how a judge must go about determining custody; and, under what circumstances parental rights can be limited or terminated. This means that a parent in one state might enjoy more or different rights than a parent in another state.

While it is true that rights vary from state to state, there are three things that are fairly consistent throughout this country:

1. parents have a right to a relationship with their children, either in the form of custody or visitation;

2. parents have a duty to financially support their children to the extent they are able to do so; and,

3. a parent cannot abuse or neglect his or her child.

This book is designed to guide you through the process of finding out what your rights are, and then enforcing them if necessary.

Parental rights generally encompass one or more of the following:

♦ the right to care for your child;

♦ the right to have physical possession or custody of your child;

♦ the right to control or determine what is best for your child;

♦ the right to control with whom your child will associate and where your child will live;

♦ the right to decide where and how your children will be educated;

♦ the right to make health and medical decisions on behalf of your child;

♦ the right to determine your child's religious faith and practices; and,

♦ the right to provide guidance and discipline.

This does not mean that you have the right to do whatever you want with your children. Up to a point, parents have the right to exercise care, custody, and control over their children. Their rights can be restricted by state laws designed to protect children from abuse or neglect. One parent's rights might also be encumbered by the other parent's rights. For example, one parent's right to physical possession of his or her child can be encumbered by the other parent's right to weekend or summer visitation. However, under normal circumstances, parents who act reasonably will be free from government interference.

Legally, parental rights for mothers will begin at the moment of conception. An unmarried father's rights begin at the moment paternity is established, and in some instances, at the moment the father has reason to believe he is the father and begins taking action to enforce his rights (which can also be immediately after conception).

Parents do not have to go to court to *obtain* their rights—they have rights merely by their status as parents. However, they might have to go to court to *enforce* those rights, and this can be a long, uphill battle.

HOW TO USE THIS BOOK

The best way to use this book is to begin by reading the book completely. This will help you determine what is relevant to your situation and what is not relevant. A cover-to-cover reading will also help you distinguish what you think you already know from what the law really is. It will also make clear what you do not know and help you determine when you may need to go to a lawyer, the office of the clerk of court, or the law library.

Remember, the greatest threat to your rights as a parent is not knowing your rights. The second greatest threat is your failure to take action to enforce your rights. This book will help you overcome the first threat. Overcoming the second threat is up to you.

Chapter 1 looks at how being a single parent affects you and your child. Chapter 2 discusses your general responsibilities as a parent, either married or unmarried. Chapter 3 explains the basics of the legal system as it relates to unmarried parents. It can help you obtain further information about the laws and procedures that are unique to your state. Chapter 4 helps you decide if you want to hire a lawyer. If so, the information provided will help you work with your lawyer more effectively. Chapters 5 and 6 discuss legal forms and court procedures that are common to all types of legal matters relating to unmarried parents. Chapters 7 through 11 explain in greater detail the various types of legal proceedings relating to unmarried parents.

An extensive Glossary helps you understand the meanings of legal terms that may be unfamiliar. Appendix A contains a state-by-state summary of the relevant laws. Appendix B contains sample, filled-in forms. Appendix C is a list of valuable extensive resources.

–1–

BEING A SINGLE PARENT

Raising emotionally healthy and well-adjusted children is one of the most difficult jobs on the planet. It is an enormous undertaking for two parents, and it poses an even greater challenge for a single parent. However, the fact that it is difficult does not mean it is impossible. Whether the decision to be a single parent was made by you or for you, you should know that you are not alone. More than 119 million homes in the United States are headed by single parents.

FOUR HABITS OF HIGHLY EFFECTIVE SINGLE PARENTS

There are many habits shared by single parents, but four stand out as those shared by highly effective single parents.

#1: Maintain Realistic Expectations

Once you have children, life as you know it will never be the same. It is not realistic to try to hold on to the routine and lifestyle you had before you had a child. Prior to the birth of your child, it may have been possible for you to sleep in late on weekends, get your nails manicured each week, or take off for a weekend with friends at the drop of a hat. Single parenthood will require you to reorganize your plans and priorities.

#2: Know that Feeling Overwhelmed Goes with the Territory

Children are very demanding. They are a twenty-four-hour-a-day, seven-day-a-week commitment. The younger they are, the more they will depend on you to provide for their every need. As they grow older, they are more independent, but the demands they place on you will increase. The stress associated with raising children can be overwhelming, but do not despair—feeling overwhelmed is something you have in common with every other parent in the world. It is tempting at times to believe that because you feel overwhelmed, you are doing something wrong or you are not cut out to be a single parent. During these moments it is important to remind yourself that there is nothing wrong with you and that it is perfectly normal to occasionally feel overwhelmed by the demands of raising children as a single parent.

#3: Accept that the Grass is Not Necessarily Greener

Avoid the trap of telling yourself that if you just had another parent in the home all of your problems would be solved. While it may be true that some of your problems would be alleviated by being married, there will always be challenges associated with raising kids. It is a waste of your precious energy to look over the fence at your married neighbors and wish you could trade places them. Your energy would be better invested in coming up with solutions to the challenges you face.

#4: Embrace Your Circumstances

Your kids are watching your every move. If you embrace your circumstances, they are likely to embrace their circumstances. If you are harboring shame or anger about your life, then that will be what they see and how they feel.

Work to create a life you love. You and your kids deserve nothing less. This is why it is important that you continue to develop and pursue your goals and dreams. The fact that you are a single parent does not mean your life has to be stuck in a holding pattern—your dreams can still take off and fly. While on some levels this may seem selfish, you must remember that you are creating a blueprint that your children will likely follow in creating their lives.

WHAT ABOUT YOUR LOVE LIFE?

What happens if you meet someone that you want to start dating? There is nothing in the law that prohibits a single parent from dating. However, is dating in your child's best interest? That is the question the court will ask if your dating is ever an issue in a judicial hearing. Consequently, that is the question you should ask yourself before you make a decision about whether to date someone or not. If there is ever a conflict between what you want to do and what is in your child's best interest, the latter should prevail.

While it is not the court's role to tell you who you should or should not get involved with, if you would like to increase the chances that the person you are dating is above reproach, then it makes common sense to avoid the following people.

1. Someone who has a criminal history, particularly someone who has ever been charged with a child-related offense.
2. Someone who abuses drugs or alcohol.
3. Someone who refuses to discuss their past.
4. Someone who is physically, verbally, or emotionally abusive.
5. Someone who has children for whom they are not financially responsible.
6. Someone who make demands that interfere with your ability to care for your children.
7. Someone who does not share your fundamental moral and religious values.
8. Someone who does not respect your role as a single parent.
9. Someone who does not like children.
10. Someone who tries to undermine your relationship with your children.

THREE HABITS OF HIGHLY RESPONSIBLE PARENTS WHO DATE

As with highly effective single parents, there are habits shared by parents that make them highly responsible parents who date.

#1: Avoid Revolving Bedroom Doors

While we live in a society where people are free to do whatever they want, courts can sometimes be fairly conservative when it comes to making decisions regarding the welfare of children. Dating a different person each week and exposing those relationships to your children is something that could be held against you in the event you are forced to litigate custody of your children in court.

#2: Adopt the Three-Month Rule

It is not in your child's best interest to get attached to someone and then have that person torn from his or her life when your relationship ends. That is why it may be prudent to adopt a rule not to introduce every person you date to your child. It is usually a good idea to wait until you are sure about the relationship before you involve your child. How long you should wait will depend on your circumstances. However, waiting three months should give you a clear indication of whether or not it is worth getting your child emotionally invested in the person you are dating.

#3: Adhere to a Policy of Don't Ask, Don't Tell

How much information you choose to divulge about your relationship will be dictated by the age and maturity level of your kids. As a general rule, it may be a good idea to let your children be the guide and avoid offering more information than they request.

You should reassure your children that just because you are dating, his or her place in your heart and life is secure. Remind them that no one can take their place. While you are dating, set aside time to spend alone with your kids doing activities they enjoy and do whatever it takes to ensure your new relationship does not interfere with the commitments you have made to your kids.

What about cohabitation?

Is it okay if your girlfriend or boyfriend moves in with you and your child? There are two reasons courts tend to frown on these arrangements. The first is, as mentioned earlier, courts tend to be very conservative about making decisions that will impact the well-being of a minor child. Secondly, there is no shortage of news stories about children who have been physically or sexually abused by their parents' live-in lovers. Because most of these cases involve situations where the culprit is a male, courts tend to view situations where a single mother has a live-in boyfriend with greater scrutiny than a single father in the same situation. Although this double standard is unfair, until something changes, you should govern yourself accordingly.

To make this point is not to suggest that if your boyfriend or girl-friend moves in with you, you will automatically be subject to losing custody of your kids to an opposing parent. These determinations will be made on a case-by-case basis. A few factors the court will consider when evaluating whether your decision to live with your girlfriend or boyfriend is in your children's best interest include the following.

- *The length of time you have been dating.* The longer you have been dating, the better. Allowing someone you have only known for a few weeks to move in with you and your children may make the court question your judgment.
- *The age of the child.* The older your kids are, the better. Courts tend to believe that younger kids will be more vulnerable to the fallout if the relationship does not work out.
- *The stability of your living situation.* If you are someone who has maintained steady employment and a stable residence, then the court will be more likely to trust your judgment in this situation.
- *The circumstances of opposing parent.* The less stable the oppos-ing parent's situation, the better it is for you if you decide to cohabitate with the person you are dating. If the opposing par-ent is married, and is an otherwise fit and proper person to have custody, then he or she may have a chance to challenge your right to custody on these grounds.

In the final analysis, the decisions about when and who to date are yours. There is nothing wrong with following your heart as long as your child's best interest are factored into the equation. While you are bound to have relationships, always focus on you and your relationship with your child.

INQUIRING LITTLE MINDS
WILL WANT TO KNOW

Children are naturally inquisitive. Sooner or later they will ask questions about their absent parent. The following is a list of common questions you should be prepared to answer.

Who is my mother or father?

It is important that you respond to this question in a way that is both honest and will encourage your child's overall sense of well-being. Your response should not be a reflection of the way you feel about the absent parent. Your child may be satisfied with just knowing factual data about their parent.

This is why your initial response to your child's inquiries should be limited to the absent parent's name and occupation. If you have difficulty answering this question, seek professional help. Contact a school counselor or psychologist for specific guidance on how you might respond to your child's questions in a way that does not create any unnecessary discomfort or bitterness.

Where is my mother or father?

Responding to this question may be a simple matter of providing your child with information about where the absent parent lives. If it is appropriate, explain to your child that he or she can contact the absent parent whenever he or she feels the need. Perhaps you can show your child how to call the absent parent or send an email message. Encouraging your child to stay connected with the absent parent is one of the most loving things you can do as a parent.

Why doesn't my mother or father love me?

Children may interpret a parent's absence as an indication that the parent does not love them. It is important that you do not do or say anything that reinforces this interpretation. Ideally, it would be best if you and the absent parent could sit down together and respond to this question. If your child can see that both parents care enough to work together in caring for him or her, this can go a long in solidifying his or her emotional well-being. However, if this is not possible, you will need to assure the child of the absent parent's love. Explain that the fact that you and his or her mother or father are not together is only an indication that the two of you could not get along. Remind your child that it has nothing to do with him or her. Tell your child that sometimes parents may have problems that make it difficult for them to show their love in ways that a child expects. Ask your child to let you know what you can do to make him or her feel loved. Encourage him or her to come to you anytime he or she feels lonely or misses his or her absent parent and talk about how he or she feels.

SIGNS YOUR CHILD MAY NEED MORE HELP THAN YOU CAN GIVE

Children who have difficulty articulating their negative feelings may express their unhappiness through one of the following behaviors:

- acting out at home or school;
- losing interest in normal activities;
- withdrawing from friends;
- loss of appetite;
- bed-wetting;
- aggressiveness;
- nightmares; or,
- temper tantrums.

If you notice any of these signs with your child, it may be a good idea to seek professional help. The earlier you intervene, the better chance you will have of avoiding long-term problems. If you cannot afford a private therapist, then contact one of these places for resources that might be available in your community:

- pediatrician;
- church or place of worship;
- school counselors;
- department of social services;
- mental health association;
- human resources department at place of employment;
- United Way;

- teacher;
- social workers; or,
- family practice doctor.

It may also be a good idea to contact an organization like Big Brothers/Big Sisters about getting a mentor for your child. He or she may feel more comfortable discussing his or her feelings with another adult. If this is the case, do not take it personally—children often feel it is necessary to protect their parents from how they feel about an opposing parent.

ASK FOR HELP

There is absolutely nothing wrong with asking for help. Yes, your children are your responsibility, but that does not mean that you should not ask for help when you need it. The fact that you are raising your kids alone does not mean you must do it by yourself. If you have family and friends willing to offer their support, accept it, appreciate it, and return the favor whenever possible. If you do not have family and friends who can help, then your church or community center may help you find resources that can provide the support you need.

Depending on the age of your children, it will be necessary to provide appropriate child care arrangements during the times when you are at work. Leaving young children unsupervised is illegal and will make you vulnerable in a custody action. It is not unusual in custody actions for an opposing parent to provide examples of instances of how a child has been left unsupervised for extended periods of time as evidence of a custodial parents unfitness. Courts will admonish parents who fail to provide adequate child care. Many schools, churches, and YMCAs provide affordable after-school programs. If you even find yourself in a bind, do not hesitate to ask a teenager in your neighborhood or perhaps a stay-at-home parent to baby-sit for you.

You are not doing your kids a favor by being a martyr and not seeking support. The most important function you must perform as a single parent is managing your hectic household. Managing your money and managing your time are the keys to living happily as a single parent.

Money Management

If you are the primary source of income in your family, it is important that you manage your finances. Creating a budget and sticking to it can relieve much of the stress that goes along with flying solo. Other strategies that can help improve the fiscal well-being of your family include the following:

- limit use of credit cards;
- use coupons whenever possible;
- buy in bulk;
- seek quality over quantity; and,
- monitor your impulse spending.

Keep in mind that money management is a skill you can learn. If you need help in this area, consider taking a class at a community college. Also, check the Yellow Pages for organization that offer assistance in this area.

Time Management

In his best-selling book, *First Things First*, Stephen Covey, a world-renowned time management expert, offers practical advice on how to best manage your time. Covey suggests that you identify the most important things you would like to accomplish each day and then make it a point to complete those tasks before turning your attention to anything else. Covey's basic premise is simple—you will not be able to do *everything* you would like to do each day. This is why it is important to do the most important things first. When creating your daily priorities, include time to take care of yourself. Neglecting your health and wellness is not in your children's best interest. The time you spend relaxing, exercising, and getting physical exams is time well spent.

Additional Resources

Single Parent Resource:
An A to Z Guide for the Challenges of Single Parenting
   by Brook Noel and Art Klein

Money Management for Those Who Don't Have Any
   by James L. Paris

The Total Money Makeover: A Proven Plan for Financial Fitness
   by Dave Ramsey

How to Be Organized In Spite of Yourself:
Time and Space Management That Works With Your Personal Style
   by Sunny Schlenger and Roberta Roesch

www.singleparents.org

www.singleparentsnetwork.com

www.singleparentcentral.com

–2–
PARENTAL RESPONSIBILITIES

The legal responsibilities placed on parents for their children are enormous. These obligations are basically the same for married parents, divorced parents, and parents who have never been married. Parental duties are among the many factors you should consider before taking any action to establish paternity or file for custody or visitation.

The most obvious legal parental responsibilities are providing children with adequate food, clothing, and shelter. In addition, failure to provide appropriate medical treatment and access to public, private, or home-school instruction is, in most situations, seen as a breach of a parent's responsibility. However, other responsibilities may not be as obvious.

YOUR CHILD'S MISCONDUCT

Many states have enacted laws that hold parents directly responsible for the conduct or misconduct of their children. The following are examples of children's conduct for which parents are held responsible:

- curfew violations;
- school truancy (failing to attend school on a regular basis);
- weapon and firearm violations;
- vandalism;
- gang-related activity; and,
- drug- and alcohol-related activity.

The punishments imposed on parents can include jail sentences; fines of $100 to $25,000 (depending on the state and the violation); and, being ordered to attend family counseling and classes on parenting.

States have taken action to hold parents responsible for the misconduct of their children in reaction to the drastic increase in the rate of criminal activity by juveniles. Many believe the increase is due, in part, to parents' failure to control and discipline their children. Therefore, it is believed that holding parents responsible is a way to encourage them to take responsibility for their children's conduct.

There may be nothing that parents can do to avoid being held responsible for their child's conduct. However, since parents' liability is based on their failure to control and discipline their children, following these steps might minimize your liability.

- Do not ignore early warning signs that your child might be headed for trouble. For example, if your child comes home with expensive shoes, clothes, stereo equipment, etc., yet has no reasonable explanation of where the items came from or how the child can afford them, this could indicate that your child is engaged in illegal activity. Other early warning signs include a child whose grades suddenly drop, or who loses interest in activities he or she once enjoyed and friends with whom he or she once associated.

- Intervene at the first hint of trouble or inappropriate conduct. Contact your child's school counselor about guidance on where to get help.

- Keep written records of whatever steps you take to assist your child. For example, write down every time you contact social services about parenting classes or consult with the police about the warning signs of drug abuse. This information might be useful to you if you are ever charged with failing to prevent or intervene on behalf of your troubled child.

- Do what you can to prevent trouble. Spend time with your child. Get them involved in organized sports or whatever other activities he or she enjoys. Stay involved in your child's life and make sure you know his or her friends, and what he or she is doing when not around you.

- ◆ Learn as much as you can about being an effective parent. Take classes, attend seminars, and join support groups that can assist you in raising your child.

PHYSICAL DISCIPLINE

You can use physical force to discipline and control your children, as long as it is appropriate, reasonable, and does not cross over into abuse. The following may be identified as signs that your method of physical discipline is not reasonable.

- ◆ You use something other than your open hand.
- ◆ You hit the child anywhere other than on their rear end.
- ◆ You leave marks or bruises on the child.
- ◆ You hit the child out of anger.
- ◆ You hit the child while you are under the influence of drugs or alcohol.

YOUR CHILD'S DEBTS

You are not responsible for the debts your child incurs. For example, if your minor child goes out and orders $1,000 worth of baseball cards from a mail order catalog, you will not be responsible for paying the bill when it arrives. Ordinarily, contracts entered into by children are not legally binding. This means children cannot be forced to pay for items they have agreed to buy. If they cannot be forced to pay, neither can you. However, they can be forced to return the items they order.

The only exception concerns items necessary for children's health and welfare. In the law these are called *necessities*. Parents can be held responsible for paying for these items.

NOTE: *Debts*, *as used here, refers to items your child purchases. It does not refer to money that may be owed on account of your child's conduct.*

CUSTODIAL VS. NONCUSTODIAL PARENT LIABILITY

Generally, whichever parent has control of the children will be held responsible for their conduct.

EXAMPLE: William and Whitney had two children. They were never married, but shared the responsibility for caring for the children. The children live the majority of the time with their mother. During a weekend visitation with William, one of the older children took one of his guns and shot a neighbor, paralyzing him.

Parents are not automatically held responsible in these situations. Whether William is held responsible in this case depends on the following three questions:

1. Did William follow state law in maintaining the weapon? Some states require guns to be locked up in households where there are likely to be children.
2. Was the child being properly supervised at the time he or she gained access to the gun?
3. Did William have reason to know that the child might use the weapon and fail to do anything to prevent the problem?

Whitney's responsibility may turn on whether she knew there might be a problem with the child using the weapon while in William's care and whether she could have done anything to prevent it.

The bottom line is that the facts of each case will dictate the level of a parent's liability. This is why it is difficult to make predictions. You should know that both the custodial and the noncustodial parent can be responsible for their child's conduct.

DURATION OF RESPONSIBILITY

A parent will be responsible for the conduct of their children until the first occurrence of one of the following events.

♦ The child reaches the age of majority, which typically ranges from 16 to 20, depending upon the state.

♦ The parents' rights are terminated by a court.

♦ The child is no longer in the parents' custody. (If the child is not in your legal custody, it is assumed you have no control over the child's conduct. Remember, holding parents responsible for their children's behavior is based on a parent's inability or refusal to take control.)

♦ The child is taken into custody by a child protective agency.

♦ The child becomes emancipated, which means the child is legally recognized as an adult. This can happen if any of the following occur.

  • The child marries. (If a child enters into a valid marriage, most states will recognize that as the child's emancipation.)

  • The child joins the military.

  • The child is emancipated through court action. (In some states, a child can file a court proceeding asking to be emancipated. Most states have a minimum age at which a child can file. The child must be mature enough to be financially self-sufficient. You cannot emancipate a child simply by putting him or her out of your home, even if he or she is self-supporting. You might still be responsible for his or her conduct, despite removing the child from your home. You may also run the risk of being charged with neglect or abuse by the state child welfare agency.)

–3–
THE LEGAL SYSTEM AND UNMARRIED PARENTS

There are things you need to know about the legal system in order to enforce your rights and get through any encounter with the system with a minimum of stress. This chapter gives you a general introduction to the legal system. It also discusses how the system is supposed to work, and some of the realities of our system. If you do not learn to accept these realities, you will have to accept the fact that you are setting yourself up for a great deal of frustration.

THEORY VS. REALITY
Our legal system is a system of three types of rules.
1. *Rules of Law*—These provide the basic substance of the law, such as a law stating how a judge decides which parent should be awarded custody.
2. *Rules of Procedure*—These outline how matters are to be handled in the courts, such as requiring court papers to be in a certain form, or filed within a specific time.
3. *Rules of Evidence*—These require facts to be proven in a certain way.

The theory is that these rules allow each side to present evidence most favorable to their side, and an independent person or persons (the judge or jury in cases that permit a jury) will be able to figure out the truth. Then, certain legal principles will be applied to that truth, which will result in a fair resolution of the dispute between the parties.

These legal principles are supposed to be relatively unchanging so that we can all know what will happen in any given situation and can plan our lives accordingly. These guidelines provide order and predictability to our society. Any change in the legal principles is supposed to occur slowly, so that the expected behavior in our society is not confused from day to day.

Unfortunately, the system does not always work this way. The following are only some of the problems in the legal system.

The System is Not Perfect

Contrary to how it may seem, legal rules are not made just to complicate the system and confuse everyone. They are attempts to make the system as fair and just as possible. These rules have been developed over hundreds of years, and they make sense in most cases. Unfortunately, our efforts to find fairness and justice have resulted in a complex set of rules. The legal system affects our lives in important ways. It is not a game, it can be compared to a game in some ways. The rules are designed to apply to all people, in all situations. The rules do not always give a fair result; however, they are still followed. Just as a referee can make a bad call, so can a judge. There are also cases in which one side can win by cheating.

Judges Do Not Always Follow the Rules

Many judges make a decision simply on what they think seems *fair* under the circumstances. Unfortunately, what seems fair to a particular judge may depend upon his or her personal ideas and philosophy. For example, there is nothing in many states' custody laws that gives one parent priority in child custody cases. However, a majority of judges believe that a young child is generally better off with his or her mother. All other things being equal, these judges will find a way to justify awarding custody to the mother, even if it means twisting the law or the facts.

The System is Often Slow

Even lawyers get frustrated at how long it can take to get a case completed. Whatever your situation, things will take longer than you expect. Patience is required to get through the system with a minimum of stress. Do not let your impatience or frustration show. No matter what happens, keep calm, and be courteous and polite to the judge, the court clerks, any lawyers involved, and even the opposing party.

No Two Cases are Alike

Just because your friend's case went a certain way does not mean yours will have the same result. The judge can make a difference, and more often the circumstances will make a difference. You cannot assume that just because your coworker was awarded joint custody, you will also be awarded joint custody. There are usually other circumstances your coworker does not tell you about, and possibly does not understand.

Half of the People Lose

The legal system is designed to produce a winner and a loser, which usually precludes a *win-win* situation that might be possible (and more fair) with some other type of system. Remember, there are two sides to every legal issue, and there is only one winner. Do not expect to have every detail go your way. If you leave anything for the judge to decide, you can expect to have some things go the opposing party's way.

THE PARTICIPANTS

The law and the legal system are often compared to a game. Just like any game, it is important to know the players.

The Judge

The judge has the power to decide the legal issues in your case and whether you are entitled to whatever it is you went to court to receive. The judge is the last person you want to make angry. Judges have large caseloads, and they like it best when your case can be concluded quickly and without hassle. The more you and the opposing party can agree upon and the more complete your paperwork is, the more you will please the judge.

The Judge's Secretary

The judge's secretary sets the hearings for the judge, and can frequently answer many of your questions about the procedure and what the judge would like or requires. Once again, you do not want to make an enemy of the secretary. This means that you do not call often or ask too many questions. A few questions are okay, and you might want to start off saying that you just want to make sure you have everything in order for the judge. Be friendly and courteous, even if the secretary is rude. The secretary has a large caseload just like the judge, and might be suffering from stress, or he or she might just be a nasty person. You will get further by being pleasant than by arguing or complaining.

The Court Clerk

While the secretary usually only works for one judge, the court clerk works with all of the judges. The clerk's office is the central place where all of the court files are kept. The clerk files your court papers and keeps the official records of your court action. While they cannot give you legal advice (such as telling you what to say in your court papers), they can help explain the system and the procedures (such as telling you what type of papers must be filed). The clerk has the power to accept or reject your papers, so you want to stay on their good side. If the clerk tells you to change something in your papers, just change it. Do not argue or complain.

Lawyers

Lawyers serve as guides through the legal system, and as modern-day hired guns. They try to guide their own client, while trying to confuse, manipulate, or outmaneuver their opponent. (Chapter 4 discusses lawyers in more detail.)

THE LAW IN YOUR STATE

Each state has its own laws and procedures, and there may be different procedures in various counties within a state. A book such as this cannot possibly explain the details of the law and procedure of every court in the country. However, Appendix A of this book is a good starting point. It gives you the title of the set of books containing the law of your state, how the courts and the parties are designated on legal papers, and a summary of the factors the court in your state will use to make determinations on the matters of child custody, child support, and the termination of parental rights.

To obtain more information, call or visit the clerk of the court where you will be filing your case. The clerk will be able to tell you if there are any required forms you will need, how much filing fees are, where the nearest law library is located, and may give you limited guidance through the court procedures. The clerk may also provide forms for you to use. Such forms may be given out for free, or there may be a small charge for them. Court clerks cannot give you legal advice, however, as this would constitute practicing law without a license. The amount of assistance you will obtain from a clerk will vary from court to court, from no assistance at all to a lot of valuable help.

It is also strongly suggested that you visit a law library. These are usually located in or near the courthouse. Law libraries may also be found at law schools. Law libraries may have limitations on who is allowed to use them (for example, county law libraries may only be open to members of the bar, and law school libraries may only be open to students and faculty), or the times when they may be open to the general public may be limited. However, in most locations, county law libraries and state-supported law schools will be available to you. The next section of this chapter will help you find what you need at the law library.

LEGAL RESEARCH

To be certain you are doing things correctly, you might need to do a little research. You may want to visit a local law library. One can usually be found in or near your county courthouse. If you live near a law school, you can also find a law library there. The public library might also have copies of your state statutes or code.

Statutes or Code

The main source of information will be the set of volumes that contains the laws passed by your state legislature. Depending upon your state, these will be referred to as either the statutes or the code of your state. (For example, the North Carolina General Statutes or the Mississippi Code). Appendix A includes the title of the set of laws for each state. Ask the law librarian for help if you have any problems locating your state's statutes or code. Each year the state legislatures meet and change the law; therefore, it is important to be sure you have the most current version.

> ## PARENT TIP
> _____
> Do not hesitate to ask a librarian to help you find what you need. A librarian cannot give you legal advice, but can show you where to find your state's laws and other books on the type of case you are filing.

Nearly every state makes available online its statutes or code. If you go to the official website for your state, you can usually find a link to the statutes or code. You can also go online to **www.findlaw.com**. This site provides each state's laws as well. Simply navigate through the site to your state and the information you need.

Practice Manuals

At the law library, you will also be able to find books containing detailed information about the laws in your state, some of which may include sample forms. Some of these books are written in connection with continuing education seminars for lawyers. They can be very helpful in answering your questions about specific situations.

Court Rules

Court rules or procedures are those that are applied in the courts of your state. They might also contain some approved forms. You probably will not need to use the court rules, but they might be helpful if the court clerk or judge tells you that you have not done something right. In such a case, you might need to read the rule to find out how to correct the problem.

You probably will not need to do anymore research than to look up the law provisions in your state's statutes or code and look at some forms in a form or procedure book. However, just in case you need (or want) to go further with your research, some information to help you is provided. In addition to the laws passed by the legislature, law is also made by the decisions of the judges in various cases each year. To find this case law, you will need to go to a law library. In addition to annotated codes or statutes, there are several types of books used to find case law.

Digests

A *digest* is a set of volumes that gives short summaries of appeals court cases and directs you to where you can find the court's full written opinion. The information in the digest is arranged alphabetically by subject. When you locate the digest for your state (such as *New York Digest*), look in the index to find the chapter to which you should refer.

Case Reporters

Case reporters are where the appeals courts publish their written opinions on the cases they hear. There might be a specific reporter for your state or you might need to use a regional reporter that contains cases from several states in your area. There might be two or even three series of the regional reporter, the later series being newer than the first. For example, if the digest tells you that the case of *Smith v. Smith* is located at 149 So.2d 721, you can find the case by going to Volume 149 of the *Southern Reporter 2d Series* and turning to page 721. In its opinion, the court will discuss what the case was about, what questions of law were presented for consideration, and what the court decided and why.

Legal Encyclopedia

A *legal encyclopedia* is similar to a regular encyclopedia. You simply look up the subject you want, such as "paternity," and it gives you a summary of the law on that subject. It will also refer you to specific court cases that can then be found in the reporter. On a national level, the two main sets of legal encyclopedias are *American Jurisprudence* (Am. Jur.) and *Corpus Juris Secundum* (C.J.S.). You might also find a set for your state, such as the *Texas Jurisprudence*.

–4–
HIRING AN ATTORNEY

Whether or not you need an attorney will depend upon many factors, such as how comfortable you feel handling the matter yourself, whether your situation is more complicated than usual, and how much opposition you get from the opposing party or the opposing party's attorney. It might also be advisable to hire an attorney if you encounter a judge with a hostile attitude.

DO YOU WANT A LAWYER?
One of the first questions you will want to consider, and most likely one of the reasons you are reading this book is to answer the question, *how much will an attorney cost?*

Attorneys come in all ages, shapes, sizes, sexes, racial, and ethnic groups—and price ranges. Lawyers usually charge an hourly rate ranging from about $75 to $300 per hour. Of course, these fees vary from state to state. Most new attorneys are less expensive and are quite capable of handling simple matters. However, if your situation is complicated, you may feel more comfortable with a more experienced lawyer.

Another question many people have is, *can I get a court-appointed lawyer*? A court-appointed lawyer is a

---

PARENT TIP

A very general rule is that you should consider hiring an attorney whenever you reach a point where you no longer feel comfortable representing yourself. This point will vary greatly with each person, so there is no easy way to be more definite.

lawyer the judge appoints to represent a party in a court action. Generally, the court will only appoint a lawyer to represent people who have been charged with a crime and who cannot afford an attorney. However, in some states, the court may also appoint an attorney to represent people in the following situations:

♦ a parent who is subject to having their parental rights terminated;
♦ a man who has been served with a paternity action; or,
♦ a parent facing criminal charges relating to the failure to pay child support.

It is important to note that a court-appointed lawyer is not necessarily free. You may be responsible for reimbursing the state for the cost of the attorney. However, you can expect the fee will be less than what you would pay for hiring an attorney on your own.

Advantages to Hiring a Lawyer

The following are some of the advantages to hiring a lawyer.

♦ Judges and other attorneys might take you more seriously. Most judges prefer that both parties have attorneys. They feel this helps the case move in a more orderly fashion because both sides will know the procedures and relevant issues. People representing themselves very often waste time on matters that have absolutely no bearing on the outcome of the case.
♦ A lawyer will serve as a buffer between you and the opposing party, leading to a quicker passage through the legal system by reducing the chance for emotions to take control and confuse issues.
♦ Attorneys prefer to deal with other attorneys for the same reasons judges prefer both parties to have lawyers. However, if you become familiar with this book and conduct yourself in a calm and proper manner, you should have no trouble.
♦ You can let your attorney worry about all of the details. By having an attorney, you only need to become generally familiar with the contents of this book. It will be your attorney's job to file the proper papers in the correct form and to deal with the

clerks, the judge, the sheriff, the opposing party, and the opposing party's attorney.

◆ Lawyers provide professional assistance with problems. It is an advantage to have an attorney if your case is complicated or suddenly becomes complicated. It can also be comforting to have a lawyer to turn to for advice and to answer questions.

Advantages to Representing Yourself

The following are some advantages to representing yourself.

◆ You save the cost of retaining a lawyer.

◆ Sometimes judges feel more sympathetic toward a person not represented by an attorney, resulting in the unrepresented person being allowed a certain amount of leeway with the rules.

◆ The procedure might be faster. Two of the most frequent complaints about lawyers involve delays in completing the case and the failure to return phone calls. Most lawyers have a heavy caseload, which sometimes results in cases being neglected for lengthy periods of time. If you are following the progress of your own case, you will be able to diligently push it through the system.

◆ Selecting an attorney is not easy. As the section on "Selecting a Lawyer" shows, it is hard to know whether you are selecting an attorney with whom you will be comfortable.

Middle Ground

You may want to look for an attorney who is willing to accept an hourly fee to answer your questions and give you help when you need assistance. This will save you some legal costs but still allow you to obtain some professional advice. Just be aware that lawyers often find fault with anything they did not personally prepare. A lawyer might tell you that you have done everything wrong and try to persuade you to have him or her handle your case entirely. You might want to see a lawyer only if you have encountered a problem at the clerk's office or with the judge.

SELECTING AN ATTORNEY

This is a two-step process. First, you need to decide which attorney with whom to make an appointment. Then, you need to decide if you want to hire that attorney.

Finding Lawyers

The following are some suggestions to help you locate lawyers for further consideration.

- *A friend.* A common and frequently the best way to find a lawyer is to ask someone you know to recommend one. This is especially helpful if the lawyer represented your friend in a similar matter.

- *Attorney referral service.* You can find one by looking in the Yellow Pages under "Attorney Referral Service" or "Attorneys." This service is usually provided by the state or county bar association, and is designed to match a client with an attorney handling cases in the area of law the client needs. The referral service does not guarantee the quality of work nor the level of experience or ability of the attorney. Finding a lawyer this way will at least connect you with one who is interested in family law matters and who probably has some experience in that area.

- *Yellow Pages.* Check under the heading "Attorneys" in the Yellow Pages. Many of the lawyers and law firms will place display ads here indicating their areas of practice and educational backgrounds. Look for ads for firms or lawyers that indicate they practice "family law" or "domestic relations."

- *Another lawyer.* If you have used the services of an attorney in the past for some other matter (for example, a real estate closing, traffic ticket, or will), you might want to ask him or her if he or she handles family law matters or could refer you to an attorney whose ability is respected in the area of family law.

Evaluating a Lawyer

Select three to five attorneys worthy of further consideration. Call each attorney's office, explain that you are interested in seeking assistance, and ask the following the questions.

- ◆ Does the attorney (or firm) handle the type of case in which you are involved?
- ◆ How much can you expect it to cost?
- ◆ How soon can you get an appointment?

If you like the answers you get, ask if you can speak to the attorney. Some offices will permit this, but others will require you to make an appointment. Make the appointment if that is required. Once you get in contact with the attorney (either on the phone or at the appointment), ask the following questions.

- ◆ How much will it cost?
- ◆ How will the fee be paid?
- ◆ How long has the attorney been in practice?
- ◆ How long has the attorney been in practice in your state?
- ◆ What percentage of the attorney's cases involve family law matters? (Do not expect an exact answer, but you should get a rough estimate that is at least 20%.)
- ◆ How long will it take? (Again, do not expect an exact answer, but the attorney should be able to give you an average range and discuss things that might make a difference.)

If you get acceptable answers to these questions, it is time to ask yourself the following questions about the lawyer.

- ◆ Do you feel comfortable talking to the lawyer?
- ◆ Is the lawyer friendly toward you?
- ◆ Does the lawyer seem confident in him- or herself?
- ◆ Does the lawyer seem to be straightforward with you and able to explain things so you understand?

If you get satisfactory answers to all of these questions, you probably have a lawyer with whom you will be able to work. Most clients are happy with an attorney with whom they feel comfortable.

WORKING WITH AN ATTORNEY

You will work best with your attorney if you keep an open, honest, and friendly attitude. Also consider the following suggestions.

Ask Questions

If you want to know something or if you do not understand something, ask your attorney. If you do not understand the answer, ask your lawyer to explain it again. There are many points of law that even lawyers do not fully understand, so do not be embarrassed to ask questions. Many people who say they had a bad experience with a lawyer either did not ask enough questions or had a lawyer who would not take the time to explain things to them. If your lawyer is not taking the time to explain what he or she is doing, it might be time to look for a new lawyer.

Complete Information

Give your lawyer complete information—anything you tell your attorney is confidential. An attorney can lose his or her license to practice if he or she reveals information without your permission, so do not hold back. Tell your lawyer everything, even if it does not seem important to you. There are many things that seem unimportant to people who are not lawyers, but can change the outcome of a case. Do not keep something back because you are afraid it will hurt your case. Your case can be damaged if your lawyer does not find out about something until he or she hears it in court from the opposing party's attorney. By knowing in advance, he or she can plan to eliminate or reduce the damage to your case.

Accept Reality

Listen to what your lawyer tells you about the law and the system, and accept it. It will do you no good to argue because the law or the system does not work the way you think it should. For example, if your lawyer tells you that the judge cannot hear your case for two weeks, do not try demanding that a hearing be set for tomorrow. By refusing to accept reality, you are only setting yourself up for disappointment. (Keep in mind that it is not your attorney's fault that the system is not perfect.)

Be Patient

Be patient in your dealings with the system (which is often slow) as well as with your attorney. Do not expect your lawyer to return your phone call within an hour. He or she might not be able to return it the same day either. Most lawyers are very busy and overworked. It is rare that an attorney can maintain a full caseload and still make each client feel as if he or she is the only client.

Talk to Your Lawyer's Secretary

The lawyer's secretary can be a valuable source of information. Be friendly and get to know him or her. Often the secretary will be able to answer your questions, and you will not be a billed for the time you talk to him or her. Many lawyers also have a *legal assistant* or *paralegal* who may be able to answer your questions. However, some lawyers bill their clients for a paralegal's time, but at a lower hourly rate than is billed for the attorney's time. At the time you hire your attorney, he or she should inform you of such charges.

Dealing with the Opposing Party

Let your attorney deal with the opposing party. It is your lawyer's job to communicate with the opposing party or the opposing party's lawyer. Many lawyers have had clients lose or damage their case when the client decided to say or do something on his or her own.

Be on Time

Promptness is important for appointments with your lawyer and for court hearings. Especially for a court hearing, it is a good idea to arrive early.

Keep Your Case Moving

Many lawyers operate on the old principle of the *squeaking wheel gets the oil*. Work on a case tends to get put off until a deadline is near, an emergency develops, or the client calls. This happens because many lawyers take more cases than can be effectively handled in order to increase their income. Your task is to become a *squeaking wheel* that does not squeak too much. Whenever you talk to your lawyer, ask the following questions.

- ◆ What is the next step?
- ◆ When do you expect it to be done?
- ◆ When should I talk to you next?

Saving Money
Of course, you do not want to spend unnecessary money for an attorney. Here are a few things you can do to avoid excess legal fees.

- ◆ Do not make unnecessary phone calls to your lawyer.
- ◆ Give information to the secretary whenever possible.
- ◆ Direct your questions to the secretary first, who will refer it to the attorney if he or she cannot answer it.
- ◆ Plan your phone calls so you can get to the point and take less of your attorney's time.
- ◆ Do some legwork yourself. For example, pick up and deliver papers. Ask your attorney what you can do to assist with your case.
- ◆ Be prepared for appointments. Plan your visits—make an outline of what you want to discuss and what question you want to ask, get to the point, and have all related papers with you.

Paying Your Bill
No client gets prompt attention like a client who pays on time. However, you are entitled to an itemized bill, showing what the attorney did and how much time it took. Many attorneys will have you sign an agreement that states how you will be charged, what is included in the hourly fee, and what is extra. Review your bill carefully.

FIRING YOUR LAWYER
If you find that you can no longer work with your lawyer, or do not trust your lawyer, it is time to go at it alone or get a new attorney.

You will need to send your lawyer a letter stating that you no longer desire his or her services, and are discharging him or her from your case. Also, state that you will be coming by his or her office the following day to pick up your file. If he or she refuses to give out your file, for any reason, contact your state's bar association about filing a complaint or grievance against the lawyer. Of course, you will need to settle any remaining fees charged.

–5–
COURT PROCEDURES

If you decide to hire an attorney, he or she will perform the next three steps in the process:
1. preparing the legal forms;
2. filing the forms with the court clerk; and,
3. notifying the opposing party.

However, if you decide *not* to hire an attorney, then you can enforce your rights by representing yourself. You will need to initiate the legal action by preparing and filing the necessary legal forms.

LEGAL FORMS
There is nothing magical about legal forms. They are simply a way of communicating information to the court. Appendix B contains various sample forms for you to use. The forms you use must meet the requirements of your court.

Case Style
Legal forms begin with the identification of the court and the names of the parties. This part of the form is called the *caption* or *case style*. Once your case is assigned a case number by the court clerk,

PARENT TIP

Visit the court clerk's office. Tell the clerk that you would like to see a file of the type of case you are filing. These files are usually open to the public, and you should be allowed to look at one. You will want to copy the format of the papers in these files as closely as possible.

the case number will also become part of the case style. The information for your state in Appendix A will help you determine the proper case style. This will include how the court and the parties are designated. You should also look at how case styles have been set up in the files you review at the court clerk's office. Below is an example of a case style for a fictional state.

STATE OF SUPERIOR
IN THE CIRCUIT COURT OF THE FOURTH JUDICIAL CIRCUIT,
IN AND FOR MONROE COUNTY

_____Timothy Jones_____,

                         Petitioner,   Custody Complaint

and

                                     Case No. _____

_____Jacqueline Jones_____,

                         Respondent.

The case style will vary, depending upon the state in which you live. The title of the court will be different in each state. For example, in California the court will be "Superior Court of California, County of _____" (you will need to fill in the name of the county where you are filing your case). Some states just list the name of the county, while others have the state geographically divided into numbered circuits or divisions. The listing for your state in Appendix A will tell you how the courts are designated in your state.

Any blank spaces will need to be filled in with the proper county or judicial circuit number (or both). If the circuit number needs to be filled in, it will often be written out instead of using a numeral (e.g., "Fourth," not "4th"). A few states also call the courts by a different name in various counties. Do not forget to go to the clerk's office and ask to see another person's file. Look in the file, notice how the case style is arranged, and then use the same format in your papers. If you have any questions about the proper case style, ask the court clerk. Case styles are usually established by court rules.

Parties are the people involved in the case. Different states refer to the parties in various ways. The two most common ways of referring to the parties in a case are as the plaintiff and defendant or the petitioner and respondent. Again, do not forget to look at someone else's file at the court clerk's office to see what you should use.

Printed forms are preferred by judges, and gives a much more professional appearance than handwritten forms. If you do not own a computer or a typewriter, borrow one from a friend, or ask if one is available at your local library or court clerk's office. If typing is not possible, ask the court clerk if forms filled in by hand will be accepted. If so, print the information and be sure that your writing can be easily read.

THE COMPLAINT OR PETITION

The basic paper you file to begin the legal process is called a *Complaint* or *Petition*, depending upon the state and the type of case. The title may vary from state to state for a particular type of case. For example, one state may call it a *Complaint for Paternity*, another state may call it a *Petition for Paternity*, and still another state may call it a *Petition to Establish Paternity*.

Even within a state, the title may vary depending upon the type of case. For example, you may file a Complaint in a paternity case (*Complaint for Paternity*), but a Petition in a custody case (*Petition for Custody*). In this book, the words Complaint and Petition will be used interchangeably; however, be sure to use the correct name used in your state for the type of case you will file.

Appendix B includes sample Complaints for:
- paternity;
- custody;
- visitation;
- child support; and,
- termination of parental rights.

More specific information about each type of Complaint is given in the chapter about that particular type of case. The following is general information that is usually applicable to any type of Complaint.

A Complaint identifies the court and the parties, states the facts that one party claims entitle him or her to some type of judgment, and asks the court to grant that judgment.

Identifying the court and the parties is the purpose of the case style, which was discussed earlier in this chapter. The person who is filing the case is called the *plaintiff* (or sometimes the *complainant*) in a Complaint and the *petitioner* in a Petition. The person who is being sued is usually called the *defendant* in a Complaint and the *respondent* in a Petition.

What information is required to be in the main body of the Complaint is usually set forth in the state's statutes or code. This information will vary depending upon the type of case. For example, the statute relating to paternity cases will state what information must be included in a *Complaint for Paternity*, and the custody statutes will tell what information must be in a *Complaint for Custody*.

SUMMONS

A *Summons* is a legal document that is required to be delivered (along with the Complaint) to the person being sued. The purpose of the Summons is to make it clear to the person being sued that he or she has certain obligations and rights. In all states, the Summons advises the person that he or she is being sued, that he or she must file some kind of *response* to the Complaint within a certain number of days, and that if a response is not filed, he or she may lose the case by *default*. The Summons may also be written in two or more languages, and may contain other obligations and rights.

Each state—and sometimes each county or court subdivision within a state—has its own official Summons form. These official forms are usually available from the court clerk, and it is required that you use the official form. An example of a *Summons* may be found in Appendix B. (see form I.) Most states have very specific requirements for their Summons forms, so be sure to comply with your state's requirements.

SUPPORTING DOCUMENTS

Some states require certain documents to be filed along with the Complaint. The following are examples of some of the supporting documents you may need.

Verification

The *Verification* is usually attached to the Complaint. A Verification is a document that you sign before a notary public. In this sworn statement, you declare that all of the information included in the Complaint is true, either because you know first-hand that it is true or because you believe it to be true. This makes your Complaint a statement under oath, subjecting you to being charged with perjury if you knowingly make a false statement in your Complaint. (See form F, Appendix B for a sample Verification.)

Uniform Child Custody Jurisdiction Act Affidavit

The *Uniform Child Custody Jurisdiction Act Affidavit* is either attached to or filed along with a Complaint for custody or visitation. This form came to be as the result of people moving from state to state to try to get a favorable custody order. The purpose of this form is to alert the court if there is a possible conflict with either a court proceeding in another state, or in another court in the same state.

In some states, the information in this form may be put directly into the Complaint instead of filing a separate form. This form requires some basic information about where and with whom the child has lived for the past few years, and whether there are or have been any other court proceedings that might affect custody or visitation (such as a case for custody, visitation, abuse, neglect, termination of parental rights, etc.). See the sample Uniform Child Custody Act Affidavit in Appendix B.

Cover Sheet

A *cover sheet* is a general term for various administrative forms that many states require to be filed with a Complaint. It may be called a cover sheet or some other name. The purpose of a cover sheet is to help the court keep track of how many cases it handles each year, how many of each type of case it handles, and other statistical information. Cover sheets are usually available from the court clerk, and can be filled out at the time you go to file your case. An example of a typical cover sheet is included as form N in Appendix B.

Financial Affidavit

A *Financial Affidavit* will usually be required in cases involving child support. Both parties will be required to file their own Financial Affidavit, which will include information about their income, expenses, what they own, and debt. This information will serve as a basis for calculating the amount of child support. Financial Affidavits are often required in custody cases also, either to satisfy the court that the person seeking custody will be able to support the child or because the question of child support is also raised in the case. Some states have an official form for this purpose, and others leave it up to the parties to come up with their own form.

Birth Certificate

Depending upon the type of case you are filing and the state in which you file, you may be required to file a certified copy of the child's birth certificate.

It is impossible to list all the forms that may be required by your court. To find out what other forms you may need, you can ask the court clerk, go to the clerk's office and look at a file for the same type of case you are filing, or do some research at the nearest law library.

FILING WITH THE COURT CLERK

Once your initial documents are prepared, you will need to file your case with the court clerk. First, make at least three copies of your Complaint and any other papers you have prepared. This will give you one copy to file with the clerk, one for the opposing party, one for yourself, and one extra copy just in case the clerk asks for two copies, or you decide to hire an attorney and need a copy for him or her. In some states, there may be another government office that must receive a copy.

Filing is about as simple as making a bank deposit, although the following information will help things go more smoothly. Call the court clerk's office (you can probably find the phone number under the county government section of your phone directory). Ask the clerk the following questions (along with any other questions that come to mind, such as where the clerk's office is located and what their hours are).

- How much is the filing fee for the type of case you plan to file?
- Does the court have any special forms that need to be filed with the Complaint and where can you obtain them?
- How many copies of the Complaint and other forms do you need to file with the clerk?

Next, take your Complaint and any other papers to be filed to the clerk's office. The clerk handles many different types of cases, so be sure to look for signs telling you to which office or window to go. You should be looking for signs that say such things as "Family Court," "Family Division," "Filing," etc. If it is confusing, ask someone where you file your type of case.

Once you have found the right place, simply hand the papers to the clerk and say, "I would like to file this." The clerk will examine the papers, then do one of two things—either say, "Thank you," and collect the filing fee or direct you where to pay it, or tell you that something is not correct. If you are told something is wrong, ask the clerk to explain to you what is wrong and how to correct the problem. Although clerks are not permitted to give legal advice, the types of problems they spot are usually minor things that they can tell you how to correct. Often it is possible to figure out how to correct it from the way the clerk explains what is wrong.

NOTIFYING NECESSARY PARTIES

In all lawsuits, there are certain people who must be officially notified. In all cases, you will need to notify the other parent. Depending upon the type of case and the state, you may also need to notify certain state agencies, such as the prosecutor's office or the social service agency. If someone other than you or the other parent is the legal custodian or guardian of the child, that person must also be notified.

The most common way to notify the opposing party that you filed a lawsuit against them is called *personal service*. This is where the sheriff, or someone else designated by the judge, personally delivers the papers to the other person.

Usually, the initial papers that must be delivered are the Complaint and the Summons. The Complaint tells the other person what the lawsuit is about (paternity, custody, etc.), and the Summons gives the person his or her legal rights and obligations (most importantly, that they have a certain number of days in which to formally respond to the Complaint).

Be sure to check with the court clerk about the proper form for the Summons, because this varies for each state and possibly even for each county. Often, the clerk will provide you with the official Summons form. An example of a typical Summons is found in Appendix B (see form I), but you will need to use the form for your state and county. If the clerk cannot provide you with the Summons form, there are two sources you can use to find one:

1. you can check at your local law library or
2. you can look at a file for someone else's case at the clerk's office.

In most cases, the files of lawsuits are open to the general public. Just be sure you look at a file for the same type of case you are filing (e.g., custody, child support, paternity, termination of parental rights, etc.), because the form of the Summons may be different in each type of case.

Once you have prepared the Summons, take it to the clerk for a signature. Then, call the county sheriff's office in the county where the opposing party lives, and ask how much it will cost to have the other parent served with the papers and how many copies of the Complaint and Summons need to be provided to the sheriff's office. Deliver or mail the required copies of your Summons and Complaint (together with any other papers you filed), and a check or money order for the service fee to the sheriff's office.

A sheriff's deputy will personally deliver the papers to the opposing party. Of course, you must give the sheriff accurate information about where the person can be found. If there are several addresses where the person to be served might be found (such as home, a relative's place, or work), enclose a letter to the sheriff with all of the addresses and any other information that may help the sheriff find the person (such as the hours he or she works).

Be sure to give the sheriff information that will be truly useful to get the opposing party served—do not just speculate where he or she might be. The deputy will fill out a form to verify that the papers were delivered (including the date and time they were delivered), and will file a copy of that form with the court clerk. The deputy should also send you a copy to let you know the opposing party has been served, but you may need to check your court file in the clerk's office.

The Other Party's Response

Once the other person has been served, he or she has a certain number of days in which to formally respond. In most states, this will be between twenty and thirty days. Read your state's Summons form to find out how many days apply to your case. The person can respond in several ways. He or she may file a paper with the court, which is usually called an *Answer* or a *Response*. (See form H in Appendix B for a sample of the form.) Such a paper either admits or denies the statements in your Complaint or Petition. Instead, the other person may file one of several types of *Motions* (such a *Motion to Dismiss* or *Motion for Summary Judgment*), which will raise some issue that must be decided before he or she will be required to file an Answer or Response.

Other Notices

Once you know the date the opposing party was served, you can count the number of days to find out when their response is due. Wait an additional five days to allow for mailing and clerk's office filing delay, then go to the clerk's office and see if any kind of response is in your court file. If no response has been filed, you will proceed to seek a *default*, which is discussed in more detail later in this chapter.

Once the opposing party has been served with the Summons and Complaint, and that party has filed an Answer or Response, you may simply mail him or her copies of any papers you file later. All you need to do is sign a statement (called a *Certificate of Service*) saying that you mailed copies to the opposing party. Some of the forms will have a Certificate of Service for you to complete. If any form you file does not contain one, you will need to complete a Certificate of Service. For a sample, completed Certificate of Service, see form J in Appendix B.

Once you get a hearing date set with the judge, you will need to notify the opposing party of when the hearing will be. This is discussed in Chapter 6.

If You Cannot Locate the Other Party

There is a way to formally notify the opposing party by publishing a notice in the newspaper if you cannot locate him or her yourself. However, it can be complicated and may require the assistance of an attorney. Unfortunately, you may not be able to accomplish certain things unless the opposing party is present. For example, if you want visitation or custody, you will need to be able to locate the person who has custody of the child in order to proceed. It will also be difficult to establish paternity if the opposing party cannot be located in order to submit to a scientific paternity test.

In most states, the procedure for service by publication involves the following four steps:

1. conducting a search to try to locate the missing party;
2. filing a motion with the court, telling the judge what you have done to try to find the missing party, and asking the judge to permit you to serve the other party by publication;
3. having the required legal notice published in the appropriate newspaper, in the manner required by the law in your state; and,
4. filing some kind of notice with the court to verify that the proper publication has taken place. (This will often be an affidavit from an employee of the newspaper, and may also involve filing a photocopy of the notice as it appeared in the newspaper.)

A word of caution before you decide to notify the opposing party by publication—if the procedure required in your state for service by publication is not strictly and carefully followed, then whatever the judge decides can be set aside at a later date.

EXAMPLE: Jan filed an action to terminate her ex-husband's parental rights so that her new husband could adopt her child. She had not seen her ex-husband in five years and had no idea where he lived. She decided to serve him by publication. Jan failed to follow the proper procedure with respect to how long the notice should run in the newspaper. Both the judge and the clerk overlooked the error. At the trial, the judge ruled in Jan's favor and terminated her ex-husband's parental rights. Three years later, after the child was adopted, Jan's ex-husband showed up and wanted to visit with the child. In this situation, the ex-husband would have grounds to challenge the termination, since he was not properly served with notice of the lawsuit.

Although there are sample forms in the appendix of this book, you should not attempt to serve the opposing party by publication until you are well-acquainted with the laws in your state.

First, you need to conduct what is called a *diligent search* for the missing party. This does not require you to hire a private investigator. However, at a minimum you will be expected to do the following.

- ◆ Contact the missing party's relatives, friends, and acquaintances.
- ◆ Check with the post office where the missing party last lived to see if a forwarding address request was filed.
- ◆ Look in the telephone book and call directory assistance in the area where the missing party last lived, or may live now.
- ◆ Contact the appropriate state agencies in the state where the missing party last lived, or may live now, to see if he or she has a driver's license or car registration there.
- ◆ Follow through on any other contacts. For example, if you know the missing party was in the military, you should contact the base or post where he or she was last stationed.

Once your diligent search has been conducted (and you have not located him or her), you should determine the following.

- What newspapers are qualified to publish legal notices? Most states have requirements for the type of newspaper that can be used for publishing a legal notice. Placing a legal notice in many major daily newspapers can be very expensive. Many communities have smaller newspapers that meet the state requirements and offer much cheaper rates.
- How many times and how long must the notice appear in the newspaper?
- Where must the notice be published? Most states require you to publish the notice in the city or town where the opposing party was last seen or last resided.
- What information must be included in the notice?

To find out this information, as well as what forms to use and what procedures to follow, you may do any of the following.

- Ask the clerk of the court if any standardized forms for service by publication are available. These forms will often include instructions.
- Refer to your state's court rules, code, or statutes. Start with the index under "Service by Publication."
- Ask a law librarian to refer you to any form books that might contain this information.
- Contact an attorney to schedule a consultation about how to serve someone by publication.

IF THE OTHER PARENT FILED AGAINST YOU

If you are the one being served with a Complaint and Summons, you will need to file an *Answer* (also called a *Response* in some states). The papers will include how many days you have in which to file your Answer. This time period is usually twenty days in most states, but may be longer in others. Do not let this time period pass. For a sample, completed Answer, see form H in Appendix B.

–6–
COURT HEARINGS

If you are unable to reach an agreement with the other parent, or if you want to make your agreement more enforceable by having it made into a court order, you will need to have a court hearing. This chapter discusses some of the key aspects of going to court.

SCHEDULING COURT HEARINGS

You will need to set a hearing date for the final hearing, or for any preliminary matters that require a hearing. To obtain a court date, you will need to contact either the court clerk or the judge's secretary, depending upon the practice in your county. If you do not know which judge, call the court clerk, give the clerk your case number, and ask for the name and phone number of the judge assigned to your case. You can then either call or go see that judge's secretary and tell him or her you would like to set a final hearing date for whatever type case you filed. Usually, the judge's phone number can be found in the government section of your phone book.

Notifying Necessary Parties

Once you get a hearing date set with the judge, you will need to notify the opposing party of when the hearing will be. This is done by preparing a *Notice of Hearing*.

First, check with the court clerk to see if they have an official form. If not, look at a case file at the clerk's office or check your local law library for the Notice of Hearing forms used in your state or county. You will need four copies of the Notice of Hearing. Mail one to the opposing party, file the original with the court clerk, and keep two copies for yourself.

PREPARING YOUR CASE

To prepare for the hearing, you need to decide what you are going to say, what documents and witnesses (if any) you will present, and the order in which you will present them. You should make a list of each fact you intend to prove, and next to each fact write down how you will prove it. For example:

- ◆ your contact with the child—phone records and copies of letters you have mailed;
- ◆ your current income—tax returns and pay stubs; and,
- ◆ your relationship with the opposing party—photographs of you and the opposing party, or a copy of an apartment lease agreement with both of your names.

WITNESSES

Selecting and interviewing witnesses is one of the most important aspects of preparing for the hearing. The witnesses you choose to testify for you will depend upon what you are trying to prove at the hearing. For child custody and visitation issues, witnesses may include relatives, friends, neighbors, police officers, child abuse investigators, social workers, doctors, psychologists, your child's school counselors, and teachers. For financial issues in child support cases, witnesses may include employers, bank officials, appraisers, friends, neighbors, and relatives who can verify your financial situation and that of the opposing party.

You will need to decide who you think would be a good witness to help your position. First, make a list of each fact you want to prove at the hearing. Again, this will depend upon the issues in dispute. Beside each fact, write down the name of the witness you believe will be

---

PARENT TIP

Have your notes ready to keep you on track at the hearing. Be sure to have your documents arranged in the order you will present them. If you have witnesses, prepare a set of your written questions for each witness. Arrange the sets of question in the order in which you will have the witnesses testify.

able to testify to that fact. Next, make a list of each potential witness, including addresses and telephone numbers, what fact they will prove for you, and what you expect each will say in court.

Your next step is to talk to each potential witness to be sure of what they would say at the hearing. Never assume what a witness will say at the hearing—find out for sure by interviewing them. Many cases have been lost by a witness giving surprise testimony at a hearing. Never ask a question unless you know what the answer will be.

For each witness you interview, you want to ask specific questions that you might ask at the hearing, and allow the witness to describe what he or she saw, heard, and knows. In addition to assuring yourself of what the witness will say, this will allow you to find out new information and will possibly lead you to other witnesses.

One alternative is to ask the witness to give you a written, signed statement of what they saw, heard, and know. Try to have someone with you when you interview the witness. That person can testify to the original statements in the event the witness changes his or her story at the hearing. The important message here is to be as sure as possible what your witnesses will say before you put them on the witness stand.

Expert Witnesses

Especially in custody and termination of parental rights cases, it may be necessary to have an *expert witness* testify. An expert witness, such as a doctor or psychologist, testifies because of his or her special education, training, or experience. At the hearing, it is first necessary to have the judge determine that the witness is qualified as an expert. This is usually done by asking the witness to tell about his or her profession and to describe his or her training and job experience.

Notifying Witnesses

The best way to notify witnesses of your hearing date is by having the sheriff serve them with a *subpoena*. It is a good idea to call your witnesses to let them know of the hearing date, and that they will be receiving a subpoena.

You will need to have the person served with a subpoena by the sheriff or someone else approved by the court. It is not absolutely necessary to serve a subpoena on a witness who is willing to come voluntarily and help you. However, if they have car trouble or are ill on the hearing date, the judge will probably not continue the hearing so that they can testify at a later date unless they were served with a subpoena. The subpoena will also enable your witness to get off work to come to the hearing. For doctors, psychologists, school teachers, police officers, and so on, it is absolutely necessary that you serve them with subpoenas.

Subpoenas should be served at least five days before the hearing, but no earlier than about two weeks. If you just need the person to testify, use a subpoena form commonly used in your state or county. Ask the court clerk for a subpoena form. Since the subpoena must be issued or signed by the clerk, they may have a form for you to use. An example of a typical Subpoena is included in Appendix B as form L.

There are two types of subpoena. One is called a *subpoena ad testificatum*, or often simply subpoena, which orders the witness to appear and give testimony. The other is called a *subpoena duces tecum*, which orders the person to appear, testify, and bring documents or other items. Therefore, if you want the person to bring documents or other items to be introduced as evidence (such as payroll or medical records), you will need to use a subpoena duces tecum.

Many states use a single form, which provides some means of designating the type of subpoena (such as checking a box or writing in the words "duces tecum"). You will need to be careful to accurately describe the documents or other items you want the person to bring. For example, if you want payroll records, be sure to use the full name of the person whose records you want, their Social Security number (if possible) and include the date of the pay periods you wish to have produced. The more specific you are, the more likely you are to get the information you want, and the more likely the judge will be willing to sanction the witness for failing to bring what was requested.

PRESENTING YOUR CASE

There are certain *rules of procedure* that are used in a court. These are really the rules of good conduct, or good manners, and are designed to keep things in order. Many of the rules are written down, although some are unwritten customs that have developed over many years. Following these suggestions will make the judge respect you for your maturity and professional manner. It will also increase the likelihood that you get the things you request.

- Show respect for the judge.
- If the judge interrupts you, stop talking and listen.
- The judge can only listen to one person at a time, so never interrupt the opposing party when it is his or her time to speak. You will be given your chance to speak and address the comments made by the opposing party after the other party has spoken.
- Direct your comments to the judge, not the opposing party.
- Talk only when it is your turn.
- Stay focused on the subject, and answer the judge's questions simply and to the point.
- Remain calm and try to maintain your composure.
- Show respect for the opposing party.

Your Presentation

The judge will know if you do not have a lawyer, and he or she may help you through the hearing by asking you what he or she needs to know, or even by telling you what you need to do to present your case. When you first meet the judge, smile and say, "Good morning, Your Honor," or "Good afternoon, Your Honor," then follow his or her lead. If the judge starts guiding you or asking questions, just let him or her control the hearing. Otherwise, be prepared to give a brief *opening statement*, telling the judge that this is a final hearing on a Complaint for whatever type action you filed, whether you and the opposing party have reached any agreement, and what issues need to be decided by the judge.

Sample Opening Statement

Good morning, Your Honor. My name is Jane Doe. I am the Plaintiff. On June 1, 2006, I filed a Complaint seeking custody and child support on behalf of my 3-year-old son, John Doe. The defendant is John's father. The defendant and I were never married. We lived together for several years, and separated when my son was 6 months old. My son has been living with me exclusively since that time.

I plan to call three witnesses, all of whom are present in court. I believe that my case will take about two hours. Thank you.

The judge may stop you before you have the chance to complete your opening statement, and just ask you to present your proof or evidence. This is usually done to save time. If this happens, submit your proof (which may simply be financial statements filed by you and the opposing party). The judge will probably swear you in and tell you to proceed. What you do next will depend on what issues need to be decided. This is where you will call your witnesses and introduce documents as evidence, as discussed earlier in this chapter. For more information about the kind of evidence you will need, see the chapter on the type of case you have (support, custody, etc.).

Rules of Evidence

Although this book cannot make you a lawyer, you should be aware of a few basic rules of evidence.

Relevancy. The documents you present to the judge and the questions you ask witnesses, should be related to the facts you need to prove. For example, if you are trying to establish paternity, the fact that the opposing party's mother became angry when you asked to see the child has no relevancy to the issue. You need to determine what information you need in order to prove the issue at hand, and stick to that information.

Hearsay. Generally, a witness cannot testify to what someone else told him or her. For example, suppose you are trying to get custody due to physical abuse in the other parent's home, and your neighbor saw the other parent beat your child with an electric cord. You need the neighbor in court to testify to what they saw. You cannot have your cousin testify that the neighbor said he or she saw the beating.

This can also apply to documents containing statements made by someone who is not in court to testify. There are numerous exceptions to the hearsay rule, and many lawyers and judges do not fully understand this area of law. One important exception is that you can use any statements the opposing party made to the person testifying.

Documents. Usually, documents must be introduced at the hearing by someone's testimony. You need someone (it can even be you) who can identify the paper, and say who prepared the paper and how they know who prepared the paper. For example, to introduce documents you received from your opposing party's employer, you can testify as to how you got the documents (although it will be much safer to have the employer there to testify).

To get a document into evidence, it is typically presented by a third party's testimony at a hearing. The document is first marked as an *exhibit*, either with a letter or a number (e.g., "Plaintiff's Exhibit 1" or "Respondent's Exhibit A"). This is to make it clear from then on to which document is being referred. Often, one side's exhibits are marked with numbers, and the other side's exhibits are marked with letters. This helps to avoid confusion.

Once the exhibit is given a designation, it is presented to the witness to identify. In the following example, the witness is a friend of the defendant in a case to establish paternity, and the document is a letter the witness received in which the defendant stated he was the father.

Plaintiff: (speaking to judge): "May I have this marked as Plaintiff's Exhibit 1?" (At same time, the Plaintiff hands a copy of the document to the opposing party or attorney.)

Judge: "So designated." (How a document is actually marked as an exhibit will vary. In some courts, you will be expected to mark it yourself. In other courts, it will be marked by the court reporter, judge's clerk, or some other court administrative employee in the courtroom. It may be marked by writing the exhibit number or letter on the document, or by affixing a sticker to it with the number or letter on the sticker.)

Plaintiff: (speaking to witness): "I am showing you what has been marked as Plaintiff's Exhibit 1. Can you identify this?"

Witness: "Yes."

Plaintiff: "What is it?"

Witness: "This is a letter I received from the defendant last April."

Plaintiff: "How do you know it is from the defendant?"

Witness: "I have known the defendant for ten years, and I am familiar with his handwriting. This letter is written in the defendant's handwriting and the envelope it came in had his return address. Since I received it, the defendant has referred to it in conversations we have had."

Plaintiff: (to judge): "Your Honor, I move that Plaintiff's Exhibit 1 be admitted into evidence."

Judge: "So admitted." (Until this point, the exhibit is not officially a part of the evidence. What the Plaintiff has done so far is to show that the document is appropriate to become part of the evidence.)

Once the document has been properly marked, identified, and admitted into evidence, the plaintiff would ask the witness whatever questions are necessary to have the witness explain what information the document contains and show how it relates to the case.

Examining Witnesses

Examining a witness refers to asking questions of your witnesses (called *direct examination*) and of the opposing party's witnesses (called *cross-examination*). One problem most nonlawyers have with this is that they tend to start testifying instead of asking questions. This is not the time for you to explain anything.

You should be particularly careful in cross-examining the opposing party's witnesses. If you are not very sure what their answer will be, do not ask. Do not feel like you must ask questions of each witness. Often it is best to let the witness go without further damaging your case.

In questioning witnesses at the hearing, you want to show three basic things:

1. who the witness is;
2. what the witness knows; and,
3. how the witness knows it.

If you are using an expert witness, you will need to ask the witness about his or her education, training, and employment history, then ask the judge to qualify the person as an expert in whatever area you need his or her testimony. For each witness you should make a list of the questions you will ask, what the answer will prove, and the expected answer to each question. Keep in mind that most judges try to finish hearings as quickly as possible, so you do not want your witnesses to get off track of what they need to say to prove your case.

THE JUDGE'S DECISION AND FINAL ORDER

At the end of the hearing, the judge will announce his or her decision. There is no point arguing—judges are not likely to change a decision once it is announced. If the case does not turn out as you had hoped, try to take comfort in the fact that you did your best. Also, because there are so many things that are beyond your control, there is no point in getting down on yourself when things do not go your way.

Whatever the judge decides will need to be written and included in a document called a *Judgment* or *Order*. In some instances the clerk or judge's secretary will be responsible for preparing the Order, filing it, and sending copies to the parties. However, in most instances, the judge will direct one of the parties to prepare the Order. If you are responsible for preparing the Order, you will need to make a note of exactly what the judge orders. Go home and prepare the Order as the judge instructed. You will then need to take the document back to the judge for his or her signature. You do not have to worry too much about making a mistake because the judge usually will not sign it until it is an accurate reflection of what was ordered.

Once you complete the Order, you will need to complete a *Certificate of Service*, attach it to the Order, and deliver it to the clerk. Provide the clerk with at least two extra copies, along with a stamped envelope addressed to yourself and a stamped envelope addressed to the opposing party. Ask the clerk whether you should sign and date the Certificate of Service. Sometimes the clerk will handle the mailing of the Order after the judge signs it, in which case he or she may sign the Certificate of Service.

–7–

ESTABLISHING PATERNITY

Establishing paternity is the process of determining who is a particular child's father. Paternity can be established by the mere relationship between the parents and the child, by the father admitting in an official manner that he is the father, or by a court proceeding.

PATERNITY LAW AND PROCEDURE

When paternity is in dispute or uncertain, scientific tests can be done. The most common paternity test uses DNA to determine whether a given man could be the biological father of a given child (tests are discussed later in this chapter). In most states, a paternity action is a civil lawsuit in which a court is asked to determine and make a ruling based on the paternity test regarding who is the biological father of a given child.

Who Needs to Establish Paternity?

You will need to establish paternity if it is not already established, and you either want to enforce your rights as a parent (i.e., to secure custody or visitation rights) or want to force the child's father to live up to his obligations as a parent (i.e., pay child support, medical expenses, etc.). The following are examples of scenarios that might give rise to a paternity action:

- ♦ a mother is certain of paternity, but the father refuses to accept responsibility;
- ♦ a man suspects the woman he has been dating is carrying his baby or discovers that a woman he once dated gave birth a few months after their breakup;

- a mother has multiple sex partners and is not certain which man is the father of her child;
- an unmarried couple wants to go through the legal formality of establishing paternity in order to ensure their child is legally protected and formally legitimated; or,
- a man has doubts about whether he is the father of a child and wants to make certain before agreeing to pay child support.

Relationship to Custody and Visitation

It is not necessary to establish paternity before filing for custody or visitation, unless paternity becomes an issue. If you are the mother, you just file for custody (or visitation) without any request to establish paternity. The same is true if you are the father and the mother is not disputing that you are the father. However, if there is a question regarding paternity, that will need to be legally established before a custody or visitation action can proceed. This almost always occurs when the supposed father is seeking custody or visitation, and the mother does not want him involved in her child's life. She will then dispute paternity, to challenge his claim to a right to custody or visitation.

Relationship to Child Support

Similarly, it is not necessary to establish paternity before filing for child support unless paternity becomes an issue. If the man being sued for child support knows without question that he is the father, there is no need for him to dispute paternity. All that would do is delay the inevitable order for support and run up expenses for scientific testing that he will have to pay.

However, if the man believes that he is not the father, or believes it is possi-

> **PARENT TIP**
>
> The husband will have to put forth strong evidence that he is not likely to be the father before a court will even order a blood test. This type of legal proceeding is complicated and should be done with the help of a lawyer.

ble that he is not the father, paternity will usually become an issue. Although some men will not put up a fight because they cannot afford the test, most will not subject themselves to years of paying support for a child that may not be theirs.

ESTABLISHING PATERNITY WITHOUT A COURT PROCEEDING

Paternity may be established simply by the relationship of the parents; however, this does not generally apply to unmarried parents. The law provides that if the mother is married at the time the child is conceived, her husband is presumed to be the father of the child. Until proven otherwise, the law will recognize the husband as the father.

In some states, the presumption is *irrebuttable*, which means that under no circumstances will the law allow a blood test or any other action that is intended to prove that someone other than the husband is the father of a child conceived during the marriage. Therefore, if you are having an affair with a married woman and she becomes pregnant, you may not be allowed to claim the child as yours even if you want to do so.

> **PARENT TIP**
>
> Particularly in states having an *irrebutable presumption*, if you are married and know your wife is having an affair, any delay in obtaining a divorce could increase the risk that you will end up financially responsible for a child that is not yours.

Voluntary Paternity

Most states will allow a father to sign an affidavit to establish paternity, which eliminates the need for filing a court action. This is a written statement, signed before a notary or other official, in which the father acknowledges paternity. The affidavit must also be signed by the mother. Both signatures must be notarized, and the affidavit must be filed at the courthouse. Paternity affidavit forms are available from the court clerk's office.

States encourage people to establish paternity using affidavits because it simplifies problems with inheritance, removes some of the lingering stigma that might plague children born out of wedlock, and avoids expensive and time-consuming court proceedings.

> ## PARENT TIP
>
> The fact that a person's name is on a child's birth certificate is not conclusive proof of paternity. There is no requirement that the father sign the birth certificate, so it is possible for the mother to list anyone as the father. With proper evidence, a birth certificate can be corrected.

Establishing paternity can sometimes go a long way toward creating a meaningful relationship with a child. For this reason alone, if a father and mother are on good terms, establishing paternity through an affidavit is a good idea. Even if the relationship deteriorates, the father's rights are established. However, men should be cautioned that if paternity is established, they will be obligated to pay child support.

Once the paternity affidavit is filed (and signed by a judge if required by state law), you cannot come back later and change your mind. No matter what information might arise to show that someone else is the child's father, the person who acknowledged paternity in the affidavit will not be removed as the legal parent of the child. If the father's name does not already appear on the child's birth certificate, the birth certificate will be reissued to show the names of both parents.

Should You Sign a Paternity Affidavit?

The best advice for both men and women is if you have any doubts, have a scientific paternity test performed. Asking someone to take a paternity test can open a can of worms, but it will be easier to do sooner rather than later.

SCIENTIFIC TESTS FOR PATERNITY

Either party in a paternity action can request a scientific paternity test. Few paternity actions fail to utilize this most effective tool. Until recently, blood samples had limited worth. They could prove with a reasonable degree of accuracy that a man was not the father of a given child. However, they were totally ineffective when it came to identifying or pinpointing whether a given man *was* the father of a child.

However, with recent advancements in the use of DNA (genetic sampling), paternity tests have become almost 100% accurate in establishing that a man either is or is not the father of a given child.

The court will not automatically order tests simply because a paternity action is filed. There must be enough information in the prepared documents for the court to order testing. In addition, the court may require that evidence be presented at a court hearing before it orders the test.

If the court orders the test, the mother, child, and alleged father will all be tested at a laboratory designated by the court. Generally, testing involves using a cotton swab to take a saliva sample from the mouth. A man found to be the father of a child will generally be responsible for paying for the paternity test. If he did not initiate the lawsuit, and is determined not to be the father, the cost is paid by whoever filed the paternity action. Prices range from $200 to $600. Check your medical insurance to determine if it will cover the cost of the test.

PARENT TIP

Because of the accuracy of DNA technology, the results of the paternity test will be conclusive, unless there is incredibly strong evidence to the contrary.

Challenging Test Results

If you believe the test results are not correct, you may challenge the results in court. The following are a few examples of the kinds of arguments that might be successful in challenging the results of the paternity test.

- ◆ The results were tainted by the lab. (You would need to prove that the lab was responsible for erroneous results in the past and that it routinely does substandard work.)
- ◆ The results were tainted by fraud. (An example might be that the opposing party sent someone else to take the test on his or her behalf.)
- ◆ You are physically incapable of conceiving a child.
- ◆ Someone tampered with the results.

PATERNITY LAWSUITS

If paternity is not established automatically, and if either parent is unwilling to sign and file a paternity affidavit, the only recourse is a paternity lawsuit. This generally involves going to court and asking a judge to determine whether the man is the child's father. This most often involves the judge issuing an order that a paternity test be performed.

Who Can Initiate a Paternity Suit?

The law only allows certain people to initiate a paternity suit. Such people are said to have *standing*. This is a legal requirement that there be a certain connection between the child and the person filing the paternity suit.

If you believe you need to establish paternity, you must first determine if you have standing. Typically, the following people have the required standing that allows them to file a paternity case:

- ◆ the mother of the child;
- ◆ the mother of the expected child;
- ◆ a man alleging that he is the father of the child;
- ◆ a man alleging that he is the father of the expected child;
- ◆ the child or the child's personal representative;
- ◆ a personal representative of an expected child;
- ◆ the mother and father of the child (filing together);
- ◆ the mother and father of an expected child (filing together);
- ◆ the state social service agency, which will usually intercede in instances where the child is receiving state or federal assistance; and,

◆ the prosecutor's office (or district attorney, state attorney, or some other name, depending on the state), which will usually intercede in instances where the child is in need of services and will generally serve as the child's attorney in the action.

If you do not fall into one of the designated categories, you cannot file a paternity case. You can go through the trouble of having the papers drawn up and taking them to the courthouse, but once the court is aware that you have no right to bring the action, the case will be thrown out. You could be ordered to pay the other side's attorney's fees for bringing the action when you had no right to do so.

If You Are Not Sure the Child is Yours

You cannot file a paternity action if there is only a remote possibility a child is yours. Paternity actions are generally filed by people who want to prove paternity, not exclude paternity.

If you have not been asked to pay child support or otherwise been interfered with, you cannot file a paternity action—even if it is simply to satisfy your curiosity—unless the mother agrees to the action. In that case, it will not be necessary to file a paternity action—you can simply use the services of a private laboratory to have a scientific paternity test performed. Such laboratories are listed in the Yellow Pages under "Genetic Screening."

Effect of the Alleged Father's Death

In most instances, establishing paternity must be done prior to the alleged father's death. There are many reasons for this, the most important being that a deceased father cannot defend himself or challenge the evidence against him. If a paternity determination is sought after the father's death, the father must have done something to acknowledge the child prior to his death. For example, the father put his name on the birth certificate, put information in legal documents, or took some type of formal action.

Should You File?

Even if you determine that you have standing to file a paternity action, that does not mean you should run to the courthouse with paternity papers in hand. There are several factors you should consider before you do anything.

- ◆ *The consequences to you.* If you are the noncustodial father, the consequences may be paying child support or the other expenses associated with the birth and raising of a child. If you are the mother, you should be sure the alleged father is someone you want in your life and in your child's life for years to come. Tying your child to an uncaring dad may not be the best action or in the best interest of your child.

- ◆ *The impact on the child.* Say that the child is in an intact family and believes someone else is their father—someone with whom they have bonded, who is acting responsibly as their parent, and who is committed to the relationship. The child's best interest should always be at the forefront of any consideration that involves a child.

- ◆ *Seeing the process through to the end.* If the person you have filed the action against resists the action, establishing paternity can be a long and possibly expensive process. If you begin a paternity action, be certain you are prepared to complete the process.

- ◆ *Handling the outcome.* Say, for example, that, as the alleged father, you have a 3-year-old who was born out of wedlock, and for those three years you have been caring for and loving this child. However, in the back of your mind, you have always questioned whether the child actually belongs to you. If you file a paternity action and find out the child is not yours, then what? Your emotional commitment and the feelings you have for the child will not go away. How will the results affect your relationship?

- ◆ *Realistic expectations.* A paternity action, regardless of the outcome, cannot automatically create relationships or act as a form of punishment. Consider this example. John had been estranged from his children. He had vehemently denied paternity for years and resisted any attempt to have it established by the court or otherwise. As he grew older, he required triple-bypass surgery.

John then decided it was time to get right with the people he had wronged. When he was ready to acknowledge his children, they were not ready to acknowledge him. He thought filing a paternity action would change things. Unfortunately, it made matters worse.

> # PARENT TIP
>
> ---
>
> The special relationship that exists between parents and children is not something that can be ordered by a court or decided by a jury. This relationship is something that must be tended to with time and attention.

♦ *Attempting to punish a parent who has had no relationship with his child.* Consider this example. Diane decided to file a paternity action. Her son was in his teens and she never needed child support because she came from a wealthy family. She had thought her child's father was struggling, but she learned he had married and had other children. Diane decided that filing a paternity action would be a way to punish him for abandoning her. She thought the public humiliation and embarrassment would cost him and his family. However, this was a painful experience that backfired.

PREPARING AND FILING LEGAL FORMS

A paternity action or *lawsuit* is a civil action (not a criminal action). The parties will consist of the person who filed the case and the person who is denying paternity. In most instances, the parties involved in a paternity action will line up in one of the following ways:
- ♦ *mother of the child v. alleged father of the child;*
- ♦ *alleged father of the child v. mother of the child;* or,
- ♦ *child v. alleged father of the child.*

One variation is where a state agency (usually either a social service agency or the prosecuting attorney) files against the alleged father to get reimbursement for *Aid to Families with Dependent Children* (AFDC) benefits paid on behalf of the child. In such a case, the government attorneys will prepare and file the forms.

Complaint for Paternity

The *Complaint for Paternity* should include the following basic information:

- ◆ the name of the state statute that covers paternity actions; (look for "Paternity" in the index of your state statute);
- ◆ a statement regarding the length of time you have resided in the state and the name of the county where you are a resident;
- ◆ a statement regarding the length of time the opposing party has resided in the state and the name of the county where they are a resident;
- ◆ the child's full name and date of birth;
- ◆ your relationship to the child or unborn child;
- ◆ the opposing party's relationship to the child or unborn child;
- ◆ a statement that the child either was or was not born while the mother was married to someone else;
- ◆ a statement regarding the status of any custody or visitation actions that may be pending or are waiting to be decided;
- ◆ supporting facts stating why you believe that you are or the opposing party is the father of the child; and,
- ◆ a statement requesting a blood test to establish paternity.

Motions

Paternity actions can also be initiated by using a form called a *Motion*. It uses the same format as the Petition or Complaint. A motion is filed when the parties already have an open case waiting to be decided by the court. For example, if a man receives legal papers asking that he pay child support, he might file a motion asking that paternity be established before he agrees to pay. Or, if a woman receives legal papers from a man seeking visitation privileges with her child, she might file a motion asking that paternity be established before she agrees to the visitation.

Summons

See Chapter 5 for information about the *Summons*.

Supporting Documents

The most common supporting document in a case to establish paternity is a certified copy of the child's birth certificate. You may also need a financial statement.

NOTIFYING NECESSARY PARTIES

You will need to notify all necessary parties of the court hearing. Exactly who must be notified may vary from state to state. The other parent will always need to be notified, and you may need to notify others such as the prosecuting attorney's office, state social services or AFDC office, and anyone else having legal custody or guardianship of the child. For more information, see the section on "Notifying Necessary Parties" in Chapter 5.

PREPARING FOR THE HEARING

The main evidence to be presented at the court hearing will be the results of the DNA or other scientific test for paternity. Therefore, you will need to obtain a copy of the test results, and possibly interview the person from the laboratory who will testify about the test. See Chapter 6 for more information about preparing for your hearing.

Presenting Your Case

The person from the laboratory who testifies about the test results will first need to be qualified as an expert. For more information, see the section on "Presenting Your Case" in Chapter 6.

The Judgment

For more information, see the section on "The Judge's Decision and Final Order" in Chapter 6. A sample, completed *Judgment of Paternity* is included in Appendix B. (see form M.)

–8–
CUSTODY

The word *custody* refers to the control or authority exercised by parents over their children. Generally, natural (biological) parents have equal legal claim to the custody of their children.

CUSTODY LAW AND PROCEDURE

Technically, without court intervention, a mother's claim to a child is not superior to the father's claim, nor is a father's claim superior to the mother's. In most jurisdictions, it does not matter that the parties were never married or that the father's name is not on the birth certificate.

Custody Terminology

Custody is a broad concept that refers to two things:

1. physical custody or control over a child's person, in terms of where they live or primarily reside and
2. custody as it relates to decision-making authority over things such as the child's education, religious training, and medical treatment.

When a child's parents do not live together, either because they have never been married to each other or because of a divorce, a court is often asked to decide the custody rights of each parent. The various state laws define and describe court-determined custody in different ways.

Traditionally, a court would grant one parent custody and the other parent would have visitation rights. In some states today, this is called *sole custody*. If one parent is awarded sole custody of a child, the other parent would not have to be consulted about major decisions affecting the welfare of the child.

To avoid such one-sided arrangements, many states have adopted the concept of *joint custody*. This may be called by various other names, such as *shared custody* or *shared parental responsibility*. In Texas, it is referred to a *joint managing conservatorship*. In some states, the decision-making aspect is called *legal* custody, and where the child resides is called *physical* custody. Wisconsin refers to decision-making as *legal custody* and to where the child lives as *physical placement*.

Some states allow joint custody only if it is agreed to by both parents. Other states mandate joint custody unless there are extenuating circumstances that would make such an arrangement not in the best interest of the child. Courts try to divide the child's time between the parents in various ways, such as six months with one parent and six months with the other parent; the school year with one parent and the summer months with the other parent; or, one week with one parent and one week with the other parent.

You should not focus on the terminology used. Instead, focus on what you want in the way of control over, and time with, your child. If you get what you want, it does not matter what the arrangement is called. For example, if you want your child living with you the majority of the time and you want input into decisions affecting the well-being of your child, you should not spend a lot of time worrying about the legal terms.

COPARENTING

This is an arrangement in a divorce or separation by which parents share legal and physical custody of a child or children. The only limit on coparenting arrangements is the imagination of the parents. Generally, parents work together to create an arrangement that is conducive to their family's circumstances. Here are three examples of possible coparenting arrangements.

- *The Whites.* John White is 3 years old. John resides one week with his mother and one week with his father. Each parent maintains clothing and toys for John at their residence. This arrangement works for the Whites because they live in close proximity to each other and John does not attend school. Once John reaches school age, the Whites will need to reevaluate this arrangement.
- *The Greens.* Kelly Green is 9 and her brother Ethan is 13 years old. Their mother lives in Oregon and their father lives in Florida. The Greens could not afford the expense of flying the kids back and forth on a regular basis, so they decided that Kelly and Ethan would live six months in Oregon with their mother and six months in Florida with their father.
- *The Browns.* David Brown is 7 years old. David lives with his mother during the school year and visits with his father on the weekends. During the summer months, David lives with his father and visits with his mother on the weekends. This is probably the most common arrangement used in coparenting agreements.

Benefits of Coparenting Arrangements

The greatest challenge associated with coparenting arrangements is that the parents will be required to interact with each other on a regular basis. This can be difficult in situations where the parties have unresolved issues related to the breakdown of the relationship. However, in situations in which it will work, the benefits of coparenting arrangements include the following.

- Both parents can be actively involved in raising the children.
- Both parents can share the burden and responsibility of caring for their children.
- Children do better in situations in which both parents are working together.
- The arrangements tend to be less acrimonious than arrangements imposed by the courts.

Who Can File for Custody

Most state laws will only allow the following people to file for custody:
- the custodial parent;
- the noncustodial parent;
- the state or county child protective agency; or,
- anyone who has been caring for the child or who has exercised physical custody of the child.

Third-Party Custody

What happens if a father who has been out of the picture later discovers that the mother has lost custody of their child to a third party? The fact that one parent has lost custody of the children does not automatically mean the other parent has also lost custody. If the father was not named as a party to the lawsuit between the mother and the third party, and he was not officially served with notice, then the order does not interfere with his claim for custody of his children. Assuming he is fit, he has a good chance of being awarded custody. In order to obtain custody, he would need to file a motion asking the court to open the custody case between the mother and the third party, or file a custody action against the third party.

Custody vs. Adoption

Some people get custody confused with *adoption*. The following are key differences between custody and adoption.
- Adoption involves and requires either the consent of the parents or the involuntary termination of parental rights. Custody decisions require neither.
- Adoptions are final. Custody decisions are never final and can always be modified any time there is a significant change of circumstances that affect the best interest of the child.
- Adoptions do not provide for the visitation of any parent losing parental rights. Custody actions provide for the visitation of the opposing parent.
- Adoptions require that a new birth certificate be issued reflecting the name of the adoptive parents. Custody does not affect birth certificates.

- Parents giving up or losing parental rights have no obligation to pay child support to adoptive parents. Custody frequently results in the noncustodial parent being ordered to pay child support.
- Adoption records are generally kept under seal. Custody records are part of the public record and are open for inspection by the general public.
- Generally, adoption proceedings are not adversarial hearings (although a termination of parental rights hearing may be). Custody can involve court hearings and heated civil battles.

Resolving Custody Disputes

Unlike other forms of litigation, the primary focus in custody disputes is not on the two parties. In every state, the guiding principle in custody determinations is what is known as *the best interests of the child*.

In most custody disputes, neither parent is unfit to have custody. Instead, it is a matter of the judge weighing the various factors and deciding which parent will be slightly better able to meet the child's day-to-day needs. Just because one parent is awarded custody (or whatever it is called in a particular state), it does not mean that the parent who was not awarded custody is unfit.

In situations in which both parents are equally fit to care for their children, courts must consider other factors—many of which are beyond the control of the parties. They often include the following.

PARENT TIP

In attempting to provide judges with a definition of *the best interests of the child*, many state legislatures have established a list of factors to be considered in making any custody determination.

- *The child's preference.* Children who are of a sufficient age (which varies from state to state) are often given a chance to express their preference.

◆ *The status quo.* Most courts will not remove children from a place where they are thriving and developing normally. For example, if a child has been with his mother for two years and the father decides he wants custody, he will have a heavy burden to overcome.

◆ *Parents are given preference over nonparents.* It is presumed that it is in children's best interest to be with their parents. However, that does not mean a parent has to be unfit to lose to a nonparent. The guiding principle continues to be whatever is in the child's best interest.

◆ *Maternal preference.* This is still a viable notion in the minds of judges, although it may no longer be the law in many states. Judges prefer to keep children in their *tender years* with their mother.

◆ *Gender.* Most judges also prefer to keep boys with their fathers and girls with their mothers, assuming that they feel that the same-sex parent can better provide the child with a role model of appropriate behavior.

◆ *Primary caretaker.* The parent who provided for the child's day-to-day care will often have an advantage in custody determinations. Usually, this is the mother, but not always.

◆ *Friendly parent preference.* Judges prefer to give custody to the parent who is the least hostile to the opposing parent. It is believed that it is in children's best interest to be raised by a parent who tries to get along with the opposing parent, as this will enable the children to have a relationship with both parents.

◆ *Relationship with siblings.* Judges like to keep siblings together. They believe this provides a more stable living environment.

◆ *Stability.* This is a major factor because judges believe children need to know where to call home. People who move around a lot are considered unstable. Instability is generally considered to be adverse to a child's best interest.

◆ *Home studies.* Judges give a great deal of weight to the opinions of social workers. In many states, courts will order the parties to submit to a home study. Social workers visit the parties' homes and observe how the child interacts with each parent. They then submit a report to the court and testify to their findings.

◆ *Smoking.* Recent reports that secondhand smoke can be dangerous to nonsmokers has made smoking a consideration in custody disputes. Although this has been considered in a few sensationalized cases, unless the child has health problems that would be affected, it is not likely that smoking will be a determining factor.

◆ *Religious views.* The parties' religious practices only come into play when the views are proven to be adverse to a child's best interest. This is difficult to prove.

Ten Commandments of Parenting

Judges look for basic parental qualities that are conducive to ensuring a child's best interest. The following factors are not engraved in stone, handed down from on high, or even put into law. Still, they are often referred as the *Ten Commandments of Parenting.*

1. A parent shall spend quality time with their children.
2. A parent shall provide for their children's financial support.
3. A parent shall provide a stable living environment.
4. A parent shall provide for their children's spiritual well-being.
5. A parent shall provide their children with moral guidance.
6. A parent shall create an environment in which their children can feel safe and free to express their feelings.
7. A parent shall provide wholesome and responsible discipline.
8. A parent shall thoughtfully consider and act in accordance with their children's best interest.
9. A parent shall be physically capable of providing for their children's needs.
10. A parent shall provide their children with unconditional love.

If Both Parents are Unfit

Filing for custody can sometimes backfire if the court determines that neither parent is fit to have custody of a child. The child may be removed from the home and placed in foster care or with relatives. Filing for custody is an invitation for the court to take a close look into the parents' private affairs.

EXAMPLE: Brian filed for custody of his three young children. He made serious allegations regarding the fitness of their mother, his ex-girlfriend. The answer she filed was filled with equally serious allegations about his fitness as a parent. The court determined that both parents had drug problems and decided that neither parent was fit to retain custody of the children until they successfully completed a drug rehabilitation program. The children were temporarily placed with their grandmother until Brian and his ex-girlfriend received the treatment they needed.

Fatal Flaws

The factors listed regarding what a judge will consider in determining custody will be given varying degrees of importance depending on the circumstances. However, there are several factors that are fatal to a parent's chances of gaining custody. The specific circumstances do not matter—if a parent is found to have one of these strikes against him or her, it will be very difficult to convince a judge to award him or her custody:

- drug abuse;
- neglect of a child;
- alcoholism;
- habitual criminal conduct;
- sexual abuse of a child;
- inappropriate sexual conduct; or,
- physical abuse of a child.

The Judge's Decision

Judges are given broad discretion in custody cases. Custody cases are rarely overturned on appeal. Appellate courts generally feel that trial judges are in the best position to determine what is in a child's best interest because they have an opportunity to see and speak with the relevant parties. No one knows this better than the attorneys. States that allow attorneys to select the judge who will hear their case give parties an advantage because attorneys know which judges are more likely to rule in their client's favor.

The outcome of custody cases are hard to predict. You will never know what's going to happen until it happens.

A court is not the ideal place to resolve a custody problem. How can a judge know what is best for a child he or she does not know and sometimes has never met? In most states, judges do not receive any specialized training in hearing custody cases. They rely on hunches as much as anything else. It might not be fair to say their decisions are often arbitrary, but that is the case in many situations. It is amazing how honest and sincere people can appear when they are, in fact, telling a lie. Everyone can show up for court with a new dress or suit. Few alcoholics show up in court drunk and even fewer child molesters admit to having committed incest. Everyone seems nice, well-mannered, and genuinely concerned about the child.

Death of the Custodial Parent

If the custodial parent dies, the noncustodial parent's rights would take priority.

EXAMPLE: Marvin and Melanie had two children. They never married and the children were in Melanie's custody. Marvin had regular visitation through a court order, which he only occasionally exercised. When Melanie was diagnosed with a terminal form of cancer, she and the kids moved in with her sister. Her sister assumed the role of the children's primary caretaker. Melanie lived three years after moving in with her sister. Marvin continued to only occasionally visit with the children. He did, however, show up at Melanie's funeral and express his intention to assume custody of the children.

In most jurisdictions, as long as Marvin was deemed fit, he would be entitled to custody of the children. His rights would take priority over the children's aunt's, even though she had been caring for them. Marvin's sporadic visitation would not eradicate his claim to custody of the children. However, the fact that the aunt had been caring for the children would bolster her claim to visitation with the children.

What if Melanie had a will that indicated that she wanted her sister to be the children's custodian? Children are not property that can be passed through a will. If both parents die, courts will look to the will for direction as to who should care for children. However, the best interest of the children remains the guiding principle in custody cases, and it is presumed that if a parent is fit, children are better off with the parent.

Marriage or Divorce of a Parent

Unless there is something to the contrary in the judge's order, the marriage or divorce of either the custodial or noncustodial parent should have no impact on the rights of parents to custody or visitation.

EXAMPLE: Ben and Abigail were never married. They lived together for ten years and had three boys. After their separation, the three boys lived with Ben, and Abigail was awarded liberal visitation privileges. The joint custody arrangement was necessary because Ben worked the third shift and Abigail watched the kids in the evening. Ben remarried and wanted to limit Abigail's visitation. The judge refused to do so.

Stepparents and Custody

If the stepparent wants custody or visitation after a divorce, separation, or death, the biological parents' rights will take priority over stepparents' rights. Unless the state recognizes the rights of stepparents, they will not have a legal claim to custody of a stepchild. Their visitation rights will depend on whether or not a bond exists between the stepparent and the stepchildren.

Grandparents and Custody

There are two ways that grandparents can enter the picture. One is if the grandparents are fighting for custody; the other is if the grandparents seek visitation rights. Many states now have laws that recognize the rights of grandparents.

In most states, grandparents have the right to file for custody or for visitation privileges. These statutes specify the circumstances under which a grandparent may obtain an order for custody or visitation. Many of these statutes only provide for grandparent visitation where the parents are divorced or where one of the parents has

> ## PARENT TIP
>
> Generally, grandparents are not awarded as much visitation as a non-custodial parent. Standard visitation schemes might include one weekend per month. In a visitation order, grandparents are not usually given any decision-making authority.

died. If there is not such a statute, or if the grandparents do not meet the criteria of the statute, parents need not be concerned with the rights of grandparents.

There are many reasons why state legislatures have moved to recognize the place of grandparents in the lives of children. With the social problems associated with drugs and teenage pregnancies, more and more often grandparents have been placed in the role of primary caretakers for their grandchildren. Because of the emotional attachments that develop, states recognize that it would be in the grandchildren's best interest to have visitation with their grandparents. Courts realize that by recognizing grandparents' legal rights to visitation, grandparents are encouraged to take care of their grandchildren when it is needed.

EXAMPLE: John and Zora had lived together for thirteen years, and have two small children. They were both involved in drugs and eventually were arrested and sentenced to three years in prison. While in prison, the children moved in with with John's parents. After three years in prison, John and Zora were released and returned to live with John's parents and the children for another year. They eventually split up and moved into separate residences. They both filed separate custody actions against John's parents. John was awarded custody, and both Zora and John's parents were awarded visitation. Zora was outraged that her visitation was limited somewhat because of the visitation that John's parents were awarded.

However, in at least two states (Florida and Tennessee), the state supreme courts have declared grandparent visitation statutes unconstitutional as violating the parents' right to privacy. The basic premise is that parents have a constitutional right to raise their children as they see fit, without interference by the government (as long as there is no abuse or neglect).

The U.S. Supreme Court has also overturned one state's grandparent's visitation statute in the case of *Troxel v. Granville*. This case does not make all grandparent's rights statutes unconstitutional, but may serve as the basis to prevent a grandparent seeking visitation when you do not want it from getting it.

Children's Rights and Custody

Children's rights is an area that is growing in consideration. Consider the following scenario, which is an example of how parents' rights and children's rights might collide.

EXAMPLE: Beth and Brian had been married for twenty years. They had three minor children. They divorced when their children were 9, 11, and 14. They went through a heated custody and visitation battle. Beth and Brian were awarded joint custody. The children lived primarily with their mother in a large metropolitan area and they were supposed to visit their father on alternating weekends and in the summer months. But they did not want to visit his home in a small rural area. In an interview during the case, the judge asked the children what they wanted. They expressed their dislike at the

---

PARENT TIP

Once the child reaches the age of 10, courts may take what they want into consideration in terms of custody *and* visitation decisions. However, until they reach the age of majority, they will not be allowed to make decisions regarding their well-being.

thought of visiting with their father, and the judge took their feelings under consideration, but he ordered the visitation.

The children visited for a few months, but the two older children then refused to go. Brian took the matter back into court and the court threatened to hold the children in contempt if they refused to visit. The children again resisted and the children were sent to a juvenile detention facility until they would agree to visit.

Relocating

In instances where parents relocate, the court is required to reconsider the custody and visitation scheme to ensure that it is practical under the circumstances. Alternating weekends do not work in situations where the parents live on opposite coasts.

Most judges will order that neither parent can relocate without first obtaining permission of the other parent or the court. This is to protect the right of both parents to have contact with the children.

Courts usually condone relocating for educational or employment reasons. However, the court probably will not condone relocating to follow a boyfriend or girlfriend. A parent who routinely relocates could be deemed unstable, and this could serve as the basis for the opposing parent to ask the court for full custody of the child.

EVALUATING YOUR SITUATION

Before filing for custody, there are several things you should consider to determine if filing is the best move for you, and if so, what is the best way to proceed.

Can You Reach an Agreement?

First, you may want to talk to the other parent to determine whether this is a matter that can be resolved without adversarial court action. If it is, then work together to draw up an agreement that is acceptable to both of you. The papers will still need to be signed by a judge and filed at the courthouse.

EXAMPLE: Don and Diane had been dating for twelve years and they had three children. Soon after their relationship ended, Don filed for custody of the children. He assumed that since he terminated the relationship unilaterally, Diane would not be open to resolving the custody of the children. Diane assumed that since she received the papers from the court, Don must not have wanted to resolve anything. Rather than talking to him, she contacted a lawyer.

On the morning the case was to be heard, Don and Diane ran into one another in the parking lot. Don said he was sorry that it had come to a court battle and Diane said she wished they could settle things. After talking a few more minutes, they reached an agreement. When they told the judge that their case had been resolved, he asked Diane why they had not worked it out prior to the court hearing. She said, "because he didn't ask."

Is a Dispute Obvious?

You should not always let the opposing party know of your plans to file for custody. There are times when the element of surprise might work to your benefit. The following are situations in which you should let the sheriff notify the other party for you:

- ◆ your child is being abused or neglected;
- ◆ the other parent has made it clear that he or she will never be agreeable to resolving the custody issue;
- ◆ the other parent has threatened to leave town with the child; or,
- ◆ the other parent has problems with confronting you.

What is in Your Child's Best Interest?

Step back from the situation and make certain that doing what is best for your child is your primary motivation. It may be helpful to seek the guidance of people you respect and admire. If your child is old enough and mature enough to understand what is at issue, ask for his or her input. Do not put the child in a position of having to choose between parents, but ask him or her what makes him or her happiest. Look at how your child is doing in the current circumstances, and how filing for custody might affect his or her life or disrupt his or her routine.

For example, if you know your child has a learning problem that requires three or four hours of parent-assisted homework each night, and you work the second shift, it might not be a good idea to pursue custody. Or, if you have other commitments that make it impossible to give your child your full attention, perhaps you should not file.

If you are having continuing problems with the other parent, you need to be sure your reasons for wanting custody of your children are not somehow tied to those problems and your anger toward the other parent. You should not do something that will have such a significant impact on your children, since they have nothing to do with your adult battles.

What Does Your Child Want?
While your child does not always know what is in his or her best interest, you should at least consider your child's wishes. The older the child, the more his or her desires should be considered. Seeking custody of a 16-year-old is probably not a good idea if the child does not want to be in your custody. At that age, they will usually do what they want to do and live where they want to live.

Are You Likely to Succeed?
There are custody battles that are so lopsided it is hard to imagine how they even made it before a judge. Do not file for custody unless you have a reasonable chance of success. Look again at the list of factors courts in your state consider when making custody awards. (See the listing for your state in Appendix A.) If you do not have any of those factors in your favor, maybe you should think a little longer and harder before making a decision about pursuing custody.

Are You Prepared for a Custody Battle?
Decide if you are prepared to follow the process to its conclusion. Custody cases tend to be very emotional confrontations. Custody actions can also be both financially and physically draining. If you are handling the matter on your own, you still need to consider the time you need away from work for filing papers and making court appearances.

How Long Should You Wait to Take Action?

When you file for custody can be important to your success, especially if your child is now living with the other parent. In most states, one of the factors considered by the courts in deciding the issue of custody is the length of time the child has been in a stable environment. Therefore, the longer you allow your child to remain with the other parent, the more this time factor weighs in favor of the other parent.

EXAMPLE: Bill and Betty have two children. They were never married and when their relationship ended, Betty was awarded custody. Betty got married, but there was evidence that her new husband was an alcoholic and physically abusive to both Betty and the children. The children complained to Bill during their visits with him. Bill confronted the stepfather and threatened Betty for three years that if she did not do something he would sue for custody. Finally, Bill filed for custody, telling the judge that the children were living in an abusive environment and had done so for the last three years. The judge asked Bill why he waited three years to do anything about the situation if it was so bad. Bill could not give the judge a satisfactory response and Betty retained custody.

Are You Prepared for the Result?

You will need to prepare for defeat, as well as victory. Losing a custody battle can be devastating. But even if you are wounded, you still have a child that needs both parents. It would be a mistake to bow out of the picture because you have lost custody. Your child deserves more. You will still need to have a civil relationship with the other parent and to function as a mature adult with the responsibility of raising a child. If you win, you need to be prepared for taking on the obligations of a custodial parent.

Emergency Custody Orders

If you become suspicious that the other parent is planning to remove the child from the state, or relocate the child to a place that would make it difficult for you to exercise your parental rights or sustain a relationship with the child, you should consider filing for a change of custody. Another alternative would be to seek a court order prohibiting the other parent from moving.

You can obtain emergency temporary custody until the court has an opportunity to conduct a hearing on permanent custody, but only if:

- the child is in immediate danger of abuse or neglect or
- the child is in danger of having their whereabouts concealed.

> # PARENT TIP
>
> You should file a custody action if the child is in immediate danger of being abused, is being neglected, or if there is real danger of the other parent taking the child and going into hiding or leaving the country. In such cases, any delay reduces the likelihood of success.

Whatever the circumstances, keeping your child safe starts with some basic rules.

- Make certain your child knows your real name.
- Teach your child his or her name, phone number (including area code), and address (including city, state, and zip code).
- Talk to your child about when it is appropriate to call 911.
- Tell your child the name of people he or she can turn to for help.
- Role-play with your child on how he or she should react in certain situations involving abuse, abduction, or domestic violence.
- Keep a current photo of your child.

Types of Custody Cases

Although there are numerous reasons for seeking custody, cases usually involve one of the following three situations.

1. There is currently no custody order, and one parent is seeking one.
2. There is already a custody order, and one parent is seeking to change that order. This can be for several reasons, such as when the noncustodial parent wants to obtain custody, or when the

when the custodial parent wants to obtain the court's permission to move out of the state with the child.

3. There is already a custody order that one parent has violated. This is almost always when the noncustodial parent has refused to return the child to the custodial parent.

Obtaining Custody

In order to obtain a custody order, you must be the child's parent. If you are the mother, it would be extremely rare for your status as the mother to become an issue. If there is an issue as to whether you are the father, you will need to resolve that question before you may obtain a custody order. This can be done either by filing an affidavit of paternity (if the child's mother agrees you are the father), or by pursuing custody in connection with a suit to establish paternity.

Changing Custody

Custody decisions are never permanent, though it can be difficult to convince a judge to change custody. A custody order can be changed if there is a significant change of circumstances in the custodial home that adversely affects the best interest of the child. Ordinarily, the change has to involve the child, not just the living situation of the noncustodial parents. For example, custody will not be changed simply because the noncustodial parent has improved his or her financial situation so that he or she is now better able to provide for the child than the custodial parent. (Such a change in circumstances is more likely to result in an increase in child support for the noncustodial parent.)

Enforcing Custody

If there is already an order giving you custody, and the other parent refuses to recognize your rights as the custodial parent by such actions as refusing to return your child on time after visitation, or refusing to return your child at all, you may need to go to court to enforce your custody rights.

Defending a Custody Case

Do not panic if you receive custody papers from the sheriff or in the mail. The fact that a custody action has been filed against you is not an indication that you are unfit or that you will lose custody. Losing custody does not extinguish your parental rights or terminate your legal relationship to the child. It only affects your legal claim to physical possession of the child.

PREPARING AND FILING LEGAL FORMS

In the vast majority of custody actions, the two opposing parties in the case will be one parent versus another parent. The plaintiff or the parent who files the custody action will either already have custody and want to keep it or they will not have custody and want it.

However, there are instances when the legal action will be between a parent and whoever has been caring for the child, such as an aunt, uncle, or grandparents. This can occur when one parent is deceased or otherwise not involved in the child's life.

The *Complaint for Custody* should include the following information.

- The state statute citation that covers custody actions. (Look for "Child Custody" in the index of your state statute.) This states the authority the court has to hear your case.
- A statement regarding the length of time you have resided in the state and the name of the county where you are a resident.
- A statement of the length of time the other party has resided in the state and the name of the county where they are a resident.
- Your relationship to the child.
- The name and date of birth of the child.
- Your relationship to the opposing party and his or her relationship to the minor child.
- If the opposing party is not a parent, state the location or status of the other parent (i.e., "the biological mother is deceased").
- Supporting facts stating why you believe it would be in the child's best interest to be in your custody. Try to do this without belittling the opposing party. If you cannot, state whatever facts you feel are needed to support your case. However, keep

in mind that you will be given an opportunity to elaborate and go into specific detail when you get to court.

Summons

You will need to prepare and file a *Summons* along with your *Complaint*. See Chapter 5 for information about the *Summons*.

Supporting Documents

In addition to the *Summons* and *Complaint*, you will probably need to file some other documents. Which documents are necessary will vary between states, counties within the state, and judges within a county. The forms listed on the next page are the most common types you will find. Also, see Chapter 5 for more general information on legal forms.

UCCJA. The most common supporting document is the *Uniform Child Custody Jurisdiction Affidavit* (UCCJA). The UCCJA has been adopted by all fifty states. Prior to its adoption, each state developed its own laws regarding custody cases. This meant if a parent did not like the custody determination they received in one state, they would simply take the kids and move to another state where they might receive a more favorable decision.

The purpose of the UCCJA is to reduce the likelihood of this occurring by requiring that courts cannot enter or modify a custody order until the child has resided in the state for at least six months, and the court is made aware of any prior or pending custody disputes and of the names of any person who is not a party to the action but has a legal claim to the child. The UCCJA requires that an affidavit containing this information be attached to all custody or visitation complaints. Form G in Appendix B is a sample *Uniform Child Custody Jurisdiction Affidavit*.

Cover Sheet. See Chapter 5 for more information about cover sheets.

Financial Affidavit. While a *Financial Affidavit* usually relates to questions about child support, it may be required in a custody case for two reasons:

1. to show you have the ability to care for the child you want in your custody and
2. to be used when calculating child support for the other parent to pay in connection with you being awarded custody.

Filing with the Court Clerk

After you have prepared all of the documents required to begin your case, you will need to file them with the court clerk. See Chapter 5 for more information about filing with the court clerk.

NOTIFYING NECESSARY PARTIES

If you are the child's mother, you will need to notify the child's father that you have filed a case seeking custody. If you are the child's father, you will need to notify the mother. If the child is currently in the custody of any third party (such as grandparents, an aunt, foster parents, or a child welfare agency) you will also need to notify that custodian. For more details about notification, read the section "Notifying Necessary Parties" in Chapter 5

PREPARING FOR THE HEARING

See Chapter 6 for more information about preparing for your hearing. In a custody hearing, you will be focusing on the factors used in your state to determine custody. These will include such things as your ability to care for the child and the other parent's lack of suitability to care for the child.

Presenting Your Case

For more information about how to present your case, see the section "Presenting Your Case" in Chapter 6.

The Judgment

For more information about preparing the judgment, see the section "The Judge's Decision and Final Order" in Chapter 6.

–9–
VISITATION

Of all of the types of legal procedures outlined in this book, visitation is usually the most simple. There are no mathematical formulas or charts to deal with, no complex set of factors for the judge to consider, no scientific testing, and no complicated testimony to be presented. It is usually a matter of you telling the judge what you want, the other parent telling the judge what he or she wants, and the judge deciding on a schedule that gives you an appropriate amount of time to spend with your child. Of course, as with any aspect of the law, it can become more complicated.

VISITATION LAW AND PROCEDURE
The law begins with the premise that the best situation for a child is to have frequent contact with both parents. The exception is when the child would be harmed, either physically or psychologically, by contact with a parent (this will be discussed later in this chapter). Therefore, absent any allegations of potential harm, you should be able to secure contact with your child, either in the form of custody or visitation. Since custody is covered in Chapter 8, this chapter will only deal with visitation. In all likelihood, you are seeking visitation, either because you have been denied custody or you prefer the lesser responsibility of visitation.

Agreed Visitation
If you and the other parent can work out satisfactory arrangements for you to spend time with your child, there is no need for a court proceeding. Such arrangements usually only work if both parents

recognize the need for the child to spend time with both parents, and can communicate and be courteous toward each other.

For the parent with custody, being courteous includes agreeing in advance upon when visitation will take place, having the child ready at the time the other parent is to pick up the child, having the child properly clothed, being home at the time the child is to be returned, and being flexible to allow for the occasional late return or other circumstances that may develop.

For example, suppose your son was to be returned to you at 5:00 p.m. At 4:30 p.m., the other parent calls and tells you that his parents just arrived at his house and asks if he can return the child at 6:00 p.m. so your son can visit with his grandparents. This is a reasonable request that should be granted, unless you have another engagement planned or some other good reason it would be inconvenient.

For the noncustodial parent, being courteous includes agreeing in advance when visitation will take place, being on time to pick up the child, returning the child on time, returning the child with the clothing and other items he or she had when picked up, calling the other parent in the event you will be late or wish to change the return time, and being flexible to allow for other circumstances that may develop.

For example, suppose your son was to be returned to his mother at 5:00 p.m. At 4:30 p.m. the child's mother calls you, says that she is running late at a doctor's appointment. She asks if you can bring your son back at 5:30 p.m. This is a reasonable request that should be granted, unless you have another engagement planned or some other good reason it would be inconvenient.

Visitation works best under these circumstances. However, it seems that very few parents can make this work. In most situations, it is necessary to come up with a

PARENT TIP

Only in rare situations is a parent denied complete access to his or her children. Even parents who abuse their children are usually awarded some form of visitation.

more rigid schedule. This can be done by the parents simply writing out a schedule and some basic rules, or it can be done more formally through a court order.

Visitation Orders

As stated earlier, it is a well-established principle in the law that it is in the best interest of a child to have visitation privileges with a noncustodial parent.

Visitation plans include the following.

♦ *Weekends.* Visitation on weekends is the most common because children are not in school and most parents are not working. Generally, courts will order an alternating schedule that will allow both parents time to spend with the child on their off days.

♦ *Summer.* Summer visitation can vary in length from one week to the entire time the child is away from school. If the child will be with the noncustodial parent for the entire summer, the custodial parent might be awarded alternating weekend visitation. In essence, this reverses the custody/visitation arrangement for the summer.

♦ *Child's birthday.* The noncustodial parent is usually awarded two to four hours of visitation on the child's birthday.

♦ *Noncustodial parent's birthday.* The noncustodial parent is usually awarded two to four hours of visitation on his or her birthday.

♦ *Father's Day.* The child is usually allowed to spend Father's Day with the father.

♦ *Mother's Day.* The child is usually allowed to spend Mother's Day with the mother.

♦ *Holidays.* It is typical for holidays to be alternated, so that the child is with one parent on one holiday, and with the other parent on the following holiday. The holidays may be reversed each year; for example, the child will be with one parent on Christmas Day one year, and with the other parent on Christmas Day of the following year. The following are other examples of how a court might address visitation over holidays.

• In even-numbered years, the entire Thanksgiving school vacation beginning at 5:00 p.m. on the Wednesday before

Thanksgiving until 6:00 p.m. on the Sunday following Thanksgiving. The custodial parent will retain custody of the child for the entire Thanksgiving school vacation in odd-numbered years.

- The noncustodial parent visits with the child the first part of the Christmas school vacation each and every year beginning at 5:00 p.m. on the last day of school preceding the Christmas vacation until 1:00 p.m. on Christmas Day.

The visitation schedule should be fairly detailed so you and the custodial parent know what to expect. Generally, what is outlined in the order is the minimum amount of visitation you are entitled to receive. The custodial parent can always agree to give you more visitation than what is included in the judge's visitation order. However, you should adhere to the order as much as practicable.

EXAMPLE: Dean and Debra had two children together before their relationship ended. Dean was awarded custody of the children. The court gave Debra alternating weekend visitation. However, Dean routinely allowed Debra to visit whenever she wanted. The only time he limited her visits to the court-ordered schedule was when he was angry at her for not paying child support on time or for not agreeing to babysit. Debra only insisted that Dean follow the order when she was mad at him and was certain that following the order would inconvenience him. The children were the ones hurt by their parents' conduct because they never knew when they were going to see their mother.

One benefit of following court-ordered visitation is that everyone will know what to expect. The custodial parent can make plans because he or she knows the children will be with the other parent. The noncustodial parent can make plans because he or she knows exactly when time will be spent with the children. Following the order will also reduce the chances of the noncustodial parent having to take the custodial parent back into court for failing to adhere to the visitation order.

A consistent deviation from the order can result in a modification, which might limit your visitation to what you actually do instead of what is in the court papers. For example, if the court order gives the noncustodial parent visitation every other weekend but he or she only visits one weekend a month, the custodial parent can ask the judge to change the order to one weekend each month. There is a good chance the custodial parent will succeed in having the visitation changed.

Progressive Visitation

There are instances when the court will make a progressive or gradual visitation schedule. Two examples of when the court will make this kind of schedule include the following:

1. the child is not old enough to spend large amounts of time away from the custodial parent or
2. the relationship between the child and the parent filing for custody needs to be established.

An example of a progressive court-ordered visitation schedule may read as follows:

```
For the first six months, visitation shall
take place twice each week for four hours.

Following the six-month period and for the
next two years, visitation shall take place on
alternating Saturdays and Sundays for six
hours on each day.

Thereafter, visitation shall take place on
alternating weekends beginning Friday at 5 p.m.
until Sunday at 6 p.m.
```

Overnight Visitation

Visitation schedules do not automatically include overnight visitation. Generally, most visitation plans do include some period of overnight visitation. However, there are instances when the court might not award overnight visitation. Some of the reasons a judge may not award overnight visitation include the following.

- ◆ The judge believes the child is too young to stay away overnight from the custodial parent. Overnight visitation can be particularly troublesome in cases in which the mother is breastfeeding.
- ◆ The judge believes the child needs time to bond with the parent before staying overnight.
- ◆ The parent who has requested overnight visitation does not have a suitable residence where the child may stay overnight. For example, a bed at the YMCA would not be considered an appropriate place for a young child to spend the night.
- ◆ The parent who is seeking visitation does not maintain a suitable environment in which the child should spend the night. For example, cohabitating without the benefit of marriage is still considered inappropriate conduct by many courts.
- ◆ The parent seeking visitation has not expressed an interest in overnight visitation.

If you want overnight visitation, come to court prepared to show the judge that you have a suitable home. Bring photographs of your residence and the room where the child will be sleeping. Whether you will need separate bedrooms will depend on the age and sex of the child. Courts will accept a teenage boy sharing a bedroom with his father, but are likely to reject a teenage girl sharing a bedroom with her father. Make certain you have purchased everything the child needs, such as a crib, high chair, or whatever is appropriate for his or her age. Be prepared to explain who lives in the home and who will be present during visits.

Supervised Visitation

Supervised visitation means that the visit must take place under the direct supervision of someone selected by the court. Such supervision is ordered by the court based on the judge's conclusion that the visiting parent poses some kind of threat to the child if not supervised. The issue of supervision usually arises when the custodial parent requests that visitation be supervised, or when a social worker recommends supervision. There are many reasons why someone might be ordered to have their visitation supervised.

- ◆ There is some question about the visiting parent's ability to care for the child. For example, the visitation by a father of a newborn may need to be supervised until the father becomes comfortable caring for an infant.
- ◆ There is a reasonable belief that the parent may abduct the child. Consider this example that involved a mother and father who had been in a heated custody battle. Before the judge could enter an order, the mother ran away with the child. Four years later, she was caught and the father was awarded custody. The mother was granted visitation privileges; however, the court ordered that the visitation would have to be supervised to ensure that she would not again run away with the child.
- ◆ There is some indication that the child was sexually or physically abused. In instances when a child has been removed from a parent for abuse, supervised visitation may be necessary to protect the child.

Various people may be designated to supervise the visitation, such as:

- ◆ *the other parent.* Because this arrangement can create friction in an already hostile relationship, courts will usually only allow the opposing parent to supervise visitation if there is no one else available to do so. In cases involving newborn children, the other parent may be the most practical option.
- ◆ *a social worker.* This person will be the likely candidate to supervise visits if a child welfare agency is involved in the case.
- ◆ *another third party.* Courts prefer people like grandparents, family friends, or someone else both parties can agree on to act in this role because the courts want to ensure that the visitation is a pleasant experience for everyone involved.

Visitation vs. Custody

Visitation is really a lesser form of custody. The time the child spends with you is your custody time. A parent who loses custody will usually be awarded visitation. The length of visitation and whether or not it will be supervised will depend on the circumstances of the case. The amount of visitation will be based on what the judge considers to be in your child's best interest. Typical visitation schedules include every other weekend and alternating holidays.

The biggest difference between custody and visitation is the length or duration of the custodial period. Generally, visitation is much shorter, although there are instances when the visitation can be quite liberal. In such cases, the time a parent spends with their child might exceed the time a parent who has joint custody spends with their child.

EXAMPLE: Dave was granted visitation allowing him to visit with his children one evening each week, and every weekend beginning Friday and ending Sunday evening. He was also given one week during the Christmas holiday and eight weeks during the summer months. Don was awarded joint custody that placed his child with him for ten weeks during the summer months. Dave, who only has visitation privileges, actually gets to spend more time with his children than does Don, who has custody.

This is an example of why you should not get hung up on the words.

Visitation and Child Support

You need to be aware of the fact that there is no direct relationship between visitation and child support. If the other parent is not allowing you visitation, you must still pay child support. Similarly, if the other parent is not paying child support, you must still allow visitation. The idea here is that the child's best interests are served by both visitation and support. Just because one of these is not being provided does not mean the other should be withheld. Your remedy in either case is to go back to court for enforcement of the court's order. The law in some states provides for child support credits for long periods of visitation.

Third-Party Visitation

Generally, a biological parent is only obligated to allow visitation with the child's other biological parent. However, exceptions to this general rule may apply in situations where a nonparent has had a significant role in the child's life and it would be in child's best interest to allow visitation. For example, consider a situation in which a child spends the first three years of her life with her aunt because her parents were unable to care for her. If the mother gets her life together and regains custody of the child, the aunt will have a good chance of being awarded visitation privileges.

There are jurisdictions that provide for grandparent visitation. Generally, a grandparent will only be entitled to visitation when there is an established relationship with the child and the biological parents relationship is not in tact. In these situations, it may be difficult to deny a grandparent visitation if they decide to pursue a visitation action. The court, in making a determination about visitation, will focus on what promotes the child's best interest. This should be your focus as well.

EVALUATING YOUR SITUATION

Except where noted, this section is written on assumption that the child's father initiates the court proceeding. There are typically three situations in which visitation is raised in court.

1. There has never been a visitation order, and you are asking the court to make such an order.
2. There is already a visitation order, and you are asking the court to change it.
3. There is already a visitation order, but the custodial parent is not complying with it, and you are asking the court to order the custodial parent to comply.

Each of these situations may require a slightly different approach. Do not forget that you and the other parent can always agree to change the visitation arrangement.

In establishing an initial visitation order or changing an existing order, you should first ask yourself, *how much visitation do I need?* The general answer is that you need enough visitation to have a meaningful relationship with your child. Exactly how much time is required for this may be difficult to gauge. There are situations when children who live with both their parents spend little time with them because of the parents' career commitments. Especially as children get older, they may tend to spend more time with their friends than with their parents. Visitation time should be measured in quality time, not a specific quantity.

A related question is, *how much time do I want with my child?* The answer to this question will depend upon your situation and may include consideration of matters such as the time you have available, your relationship with your child, and the intended activities.

Seeking Visitation

In order to obtain a visitation order, you must be the child's parent. If there is an issue as to whether you are the father of the child, you will need to resolve that question before you may obtain a visitation order. This can be done either by filing an Affidavit of Paternity (if the child's mother agrees you are the father), or by pursuing visitation in connection with a suit to establish paternity. Once the paternity issue is resolved (or if paternity is not an issue) you will need to give the judge a proposal for a visitation schedule.

Changing Visitation

The three most common reasons for changing a visitation order are as follows.

1. The child's circumstances have changed in such a way that the visitation order needs to be changed. This might include the child being older (appropriate visitation may be different for a 6-year-old than for a 15-year-old), becoming involved in certain activities, or developing medical problems.

2. The circumstances of one or both of the parents have changed (such as one moving further away).

3. The order needs to be made more specific to eliminate disagreements between the parents. The idea is to get an order that is very detailed and specific about all aspects of visitation, so that it is absolutely clear to both parents what is to take place. Of course, if the order is already quite specific, there is nothing that a new order can accomplish. In such a case, you will need to seek enforcement of the order, rather than seek a new order.

In the first two situations, it will be up to you to show that the circumstances have changed. This will usually simply be a matter of you telling the judge about the situation, and offering a proposal for a new visitation order that will solve the problem.

In the third situation, you will need to show that there are disagreements over visitation between you and the other parent. This will often be apparent from your case file, as there will be a record of previous court hearings in which you sought enforcement of the order. In such a case, it will be apparent to the judge that the existing order is not doing the job (or that more drastic action is needed to force the custodial parent to comply with the order).

Enforcing Visitation

If the custodial parent is not allowing visitation according to the requirements of the visitation order, it is often necessary for the other parent to ask the judge to order the custodial parent to abide by the visitation order. This is typically done by filing what is called an *Order to Show Cause*. Basically, the custodial parent is ordered to appear before the judge to *show cause* why she should not be held in contempt of court and placed in jail for failing to comply with the court's order.

As a practical matter, the custodial parent is rarely placed in jail. Jail only results when the custodial parent has prevented visitation repeatedly, without good reason. What usually happens is that the custodial parent explains why he or she denied visitation. This may be for a valid reason (see "Refusing Visitation" on the next page) or for an invalid reason (e.g., the other parent has not paid child support or the other parent was late returning the child from the previous visitation period).

The judge will probably lecture the parents about the necessity to cooperate for the sake of the child, explain how he or she expects them to deal with the problem in the future, explain that he or she expects the order to be obeyed, and possibly modify the order to eliminate anything that may have been unclear or not sufficiently specific. Another option for the judge would be to give you custody.

If you continue to have problems getting your visitation, it may take several trips to court before the judge will take the drastic action of putting the custodial parent in jail until he or she agrees to comply with the visitation order. However, almost all judges are more reluctant to put a woman in jail for violating a visitation order than to put a man in jail for not paying child support.

Refusing Visitation. There are a few instances when a parent might be justified in denying the noncustodial parent their visitation.

1. If the child is ill. A runny nose is not enough to justify refusing to allow the child to visit with the noncustodial parent. However, an extreme case of the flu would be enough to justify refusing visitation. If your child is ill, be courteous and notify the other parent that visitation plans may need to be changed.

2. There is a legitimate concern that the child's well-being is in jeopardy. For example, if the noncustodial parent shows up intoxicated or without a car seat, a parent would be justified in not allowing the child to visit.

3. Use your best judgment. However, keep in mind that consistently violating a court order without justification could result in the child being removed from your custody, or you being held in contempt and jailed.

Defending a Visitation Case

If the other parent seeks visitation that you do not want him or her to have, or if the other parent accuses you of not complying with an existing visitation order, you will find yourself defending a visitation case. Your defense will be shaped by the situations. In any case, your emphasis should be on what is best for your child.

If you are opposing the other parent's attempt to obtain visitation, you will need to explain (and present evidence) why the other parent should not have the visitation being sought. You may want to limit or restrict visitation from what the other parent is requesting, or you may want to totally deny all visitation. In either event, you will need to show that the visitation being sought would be detrimental to your child.

If you are being accused of not following an existing visitation order, you will either need to show that you did not violate the order or that you had a good reason for not following the order.

Considerations Before Filing

There are several things you should consider before filing for visitation. Some of the most important follow.

- ◆ The amount of time you have available to spend with your children should be considered. If you work on the weekends, having the kids on the weekend does not make much sense, considering they will be with a baby-sitter most of the time. Moreover, if you work the third shift, it does not make sense to get the children for early morning visitation if you are going to be asleep for most of that time.

- ◆ If your work schedule changes, you may need to go back into court and ask that the visitation be changed to suit your schedule. Most courts will accommodate reasonable requests to accommodate your work schedule, but not your social schedule. The visitation may also need to be modified periodically to accommodate the other parent's schedule.

- ◆ Children's needs should be reasonably accommodated. If your child plays soccer and you cannot take him or her to the games, try to schedule visitation around the games. Some children's days are filled with more activities than their parents'. Be flexible, but do not allow your children's schedules to completely dictate when you visit with them.

◆ If you live far from your child, consider the cost and time associated with visitation. If you live across the country, it might
not be a good idea to insist on alternating weekend visits. Be
reasonable and remember there is no point in asking for or
committing to more visitation than you can exercise.

PREPARING AND FILING LEGAL FORMS

You should file for visitation (or possibly custody) whenever the
other parent consistently denies you regular and substantial access
to your child. Few people are denied complete access to their children. In the majority of cases, however, noncustodial parents who
have no court-ordered visitation are left at the mercy of the custodial parent. They are only allowed to visit when the custodial parent
feels it is necessary and for as long as they feel it is convenient. As a
result, the only time many noncustodial parents are assured of a visit
with their child is when the custodial parent needs a baby-sitter.

You should also file for visitation if your paternity has recently
been established, and you wish have a relationship with your child
but the other parent has denied you visitation. If possible, you
should try to have a visitation provision included in the paternity
order, which will avoid having to go back to court, pay additional filing fees, and so on.

The Parties

The parties in visitation actions are generally the same as those in
custody actions. This includes the two parents, as well as any third
party having legal custody or guardianship of the child.

The Visitation Complaint

The information that is included in the *Visitation Complaint* is similar to that which is included in the *Custody Complaint*. The
Visitation Complaint should include the following information:

◆ the state statute that covers visitation actions (look for "Child
Visitation" in the index of your state statute);

◆ a statement regarding the length of time you have resided in
the state and the name of the county where you are a resident;

- ♦ a statement as to the length of time the other party has resided in the state and the name of the county where they reside;
- ♦ your relationship to the child;
- ♦ the name and date of birth of the child;
- ♦ your relationship to the opposing party and or their relationship to the minor child;
- ♦ if the opposing party is not a parent, state the location or status of the other parent (e.g., "the minor child's biological mother is deceased"); and,
- ♦ supporting facts stating why you believe that awarding you visitation privileges would be in the child's best interest. Again, try to do this without bad mouthing the opposing party.

Summons
You will need to prepare and file a Summons along with your Visitation Complaint. See Chapter 5 for information about the Summons.

Supporting Documents
Other than some type of cover sheet, there are generally no required supporting documents for any type of visitation proceeding.

Filing with the Court Clerk
After you have prepared all of the documents that are required to begin your case, you will need to file them with the court clerk. See Chapter 5 for more information about filing with the court clerk.

NOTIFYING NECESSARY PARTIES
If you are the child's mother, you will need to notify the child's father that you have filed a request to establish or change visitation. If you are the child's father, you will need to notify the mother. If the child is currently in the custody of any third party (such as grandparents, an aunt, foster parents, or a government social services or child protective agency), you will need to notify whoever has custody.

THE HEARING

For more information on how to schedule a court hearing, see the section on "Scheduling Court Hearings" in Chapter 6.

Notifying Necessary Parties

The parties you will need to notify are those who were notified when you filed your request to establish or change visitation. If you plan to have any witnesses testify, you will also need to notify them. For more information on notifying parties of court hearings, see the section on "Notifying Necessary Parties" in Chapter 5. For more information about notifying witnesses, see the section on "Witnesses" in Chapter 6.

Preparing for the Hearing

See Chapter 6 for more information about preparing for your hearing. In a visitation hearing, your focus will be on explaining what problems you have regarding visitation and on proposing a visitation schedule. In most cases, you will not need any witnesses unless you expect the other parent to claim that there are no visitation problems. In such a situation, it may help if you can produce a witness who was there when you had problems with visitation.

Presenting Your Case

For more information about how to present your case, see the section on "Presenting Your Case" in Chapter 6.

The Judgment

After the judge announces his or her decision, you will need to prepare an order for the judge to sign. For more information, see the section on "The Judge's Decision and Final Order" in Chapter 6.

EXERCISING YOUR VISITATION

The key to visitation is exercising it. There are people who go to the trouble and expense of fighting to get visitation, then fail to follow through on it. Their job or other commitments get in the way.

Failing to exercise the visitation you receive could result in one of the following.

- *Your visitation privileges could be severely restricted.* For example, James was awarded liberal visitation privileges, which he exercised for the first six months after the visitation order was entered. Then he met a new girlfriend and his time with her began to encroach on the time he was supposed to be with his child. The child's mother filed a motion asking the court to reduce his visitation to the time he actually spent with the child. The court granted her motion.

- *The child will not want to visit.* If he or she cannot depend on you to follow through on your commitment to visit, your child might make other plans and may not want to continue visitations. It is best for everyone involved if the child looks forward to the visits. If the visits become disruptive, the other parent may move to have visitation restricted.

Forcing a Parent to Visit

A custodial parent can probably go to court to force the noncustodial parent to visit with the child. However, it may not be wise to impose your children on someone who has to be forced to spend time with them.

Forcing a Child to Visit

A common argument made by custodial parents accused of denying visitation is that the child does not want to go for visits with the other parent. Unless there is provable abuse involved, most judges will not accept this as justification for violating a visitation order. Judges will frequently tell the custodial parent that it is his or her duty as a parent to see that the visitation takes place. The parent is to be in control of the situation, not the child.

Responsibilites During Visitation

When the child is in your care, you are free to do whatever you want with respect to caring for them. Unless the court makes an order to the contrary, you may associate with whom you choose, and you can leave the state temporarily (such as for vacation or to visit relatives). However, you must always act responsibly and maintain an environment that is conducive to the child's well-being.

-10-
CHILD SUPPORT

Providing financial support for a child is an obligation imposed on both parents by state law. Whoever has the legal status of parent, whether through biology or through the law (as with adoption), is responsible for supporting the child. It does not matter whether the parents are married, divorced, or never were married.

CHILD SUPPORT LAW AND PROCEDURE

This chapter addresses when one parent is not helping the other to support their child. If you are not receiving financial help from the other parent, this chapter explains how to go about seeking a court order requiring the other parent to contribute. If you have been served with court papers seeking to force you to pay child support, this chapter explains what to expect and discusses how you might defend yourself.

If the parent with whom the child is living applies for welfare benefits—usually, Aid to Families with Dependent Children (AFDC)—the appropriate state agency will take action to try to obtain child support payments from the other parent.

If neither parent is able to support a child, they should seek government assistance, such as welfare benefits. If neither parent provides support for a child, the state child protection agency may step in to support the child and possibly charge the parents with neglect. Both of these situations will not be addressed in this book.

A court may order a parent to pay child support to the other parent or to third parties. If the parent with whom the child is living is receiving AFDC benefits for the child, then child support payments will go to the government as partial reimbursement for the AFDC benefits. If the child is not living with either parent, then child support payments may be made to whomever has custody of the child.

EXAMPLE: Tim and Terri were never married and had three children together. Their relationship ended, and the children went to live with Terri. Three months later, she was arrested and placed in jail. Tim's parents then filed for custody. Tim did not fight for custody because he assumed that as long as the children were not with their mother, he did not have to pay child support. Tim paid his parents on and off for a while, but eventually stopped paying them altogether. Tim's parents took him to court and the judge ordered Tim to pay child support.

In many instances, regardless of who eventually receives the support, it is paid to a state agency that keeps track of the payments and disburses them to the proper party.

How Child Support is Determined

The two factors typically considered by courts in determining the amount of child support are:

1. the financial needs of the child and
2. the financial ability of the parents to meet those needs.

Most states have created standard child support guidelines. These may be in the statutes or code, or may be created by court rule, a state agency, or some type of committee. They usually involve a chart or table, a mathematical formula, or a combination of these. Such guidelines attempt to calculate child support based on what both parents earn and how much they would spend on the

---

PARENT TIP

State child support guidelines are designed to ensure fairly equal treatment of people throughout the state and to eliminate extreme variations that occur when the amount was left up to the judge's discretion.

child's needs if they were all living in the home together. The guidelines are reviewed periodically to ensure that they keep pace with inflation and the cost of living in the state where they are imposed.

There are federal statutes designed to ensure that states work together in enforcing child support awards and to keep a person from avoiding their child support obligation by moving to another state.

Many states' guidelines use the following basic procedure to determine child support.

- Each party's *gross income* is determined. This is basically the income before any taxes or other items are deducted.
- Specified deductions are allowed and subtracted from the gross income, to arrive at a *net income*. Deductions are typically allowed for such things as income taxes, Social Security, mandatory union dues, and health insurance premiums paid for the children.
- The parties' net incomes are added together to arrive at a combined income.
- A table is consulted that uses the combined income to determine the financial needs of the number of children for whom support is to be paid.
- Each parent's percentage of the combined income is calculated and applied to the needs of the children to determine how much is to be contributed by each parent.
- Any of various adjustments are made to account for special circumstances.

There are several factors that child support guidelines typically take into account when calculating child support. These may include the following.

Income of the parties. The income of each party is usually the starting point—and the primary consideration—in determining child support. The following sources of income are usually included in determining gross income for child support purposes:

- salaries and wages;
- overtime pay;
- dividends;

- severance pay;
- pensions;
- interest income;
- trust income;
- annuities;
- capital gains;
- Social Security;
- workers' compensation benefits;
- unemployment insurance benefits;
- disability pay and insurance benefits;
- gifts and prizes;
- alimony received (usually only included as income if it is received from someone other than the opposing party or the party from whom you are seeking child support); and,
- commissions and bonuses. (One-time bonuses or income are included, but are usually distinguished from ordinary income. For example, if you receive a one-time bonus of $50,000 in 2006, it will be included as part of your 2006 obligation, but it will not be used to determine the amount you pay in other years.)

Health insurance. The amount being paid on health insurance for a minor child will be included in the child support calculation. The child support payment by the noncustodial parent will be higher if the custodial parent pays the insurance, and lower if the noncustodial parent pays the insurance.

Child care. Work-related childcare costs will be included in the equation. A person paying child support usually will not have to pay for any childcare costs in addition to the child support obligation.

Extraordinary expenses. If the child needs braces or special medical treatments for conditions such as asthma or psychiatric counseling, such considerations will be taken into account when calculating the amount of the child support. Other extraordinary expenses include those associated with special schools or travel expenses to visit each parent. The court will determine whether the expenses will be considered extraordinary.

Welfare benefits. Public assistance or Supplemental Security Income (SSI) are usually not considered as income, and they are not considered in any other way in child support calculations.

Automobiles and housing as compensation. Things provided by an employer, like automobiles or housing, will generally be included as income if they significantly reduce the living expenses of the person who receives them. For example, if you earn only $12,000 a year, but your living expenses are only $300 a month because you do not have transportation, food, or housing expenses, then your income will be adjusted to reflect the items you receive as income.

Imputed income. Imputed income is the income you could be receiving if you were to secure employment in a field that is compatible with your education, training, experience, or background. Courts will base child support awards on imputed, or potential, income when it has been established that a party is purposefully suppressing his or her income in order to minimize his or her child support obligation. For example, if you are a doctor who quits his practice and begins working at a fast food restaurant three days after receiving notice that the other parent plans to seek child support, it is likely the court will calculate the child support amount based on your potential income as a doctor.

One instance in which a court will not use potential income is when a custodial parent takes a lower paying job or cuts back their hours to stay home with a small child (usually a child less than 3 years old).

Number of children. The number of children involved is considered in the equation. This may include the number of children of the person who will receive the support and the number of children of the person who is asked to pay child support. The calculations also take into account the number of children who are receiving child support through a separate court order. Money you

> ## PARENT TIP
>
> Child support is based on the needs of the child and the theory that both parties should contribute something to the support of the children.

are paying on your own, and not pursuant to a court order, will not generally be included as part of the calculation.

The following factors are generally not relevant in calculating child support:

- the age of the children;
- the age of the parties;
- the other financial obligations of the party paying or receiving child support;
- the relationship between the parties and the children;
- the financial strain placed on the paying party; and,
- the paying parent's need for the money.

EXAMPLE: Max could not understand why he had to pay child support to his ex-girlfriend. They had two small children that lived with her. Two years after they ended their relationship, she graduated from law school. She earned twice as much money as Max did. Three years after graduating from law school, she married a doctor who made several times more money than Max did.

Max earned approximately $40,000 a year and was required to pay approximately $600 a month as child support. Max's argument was that since the children lived a more affluent lifestyle than he did, he should not be ordered to pay any child support. This is not how the law works. A person's child support obligation will not be extinguished by the fact that the opposing parent does not need the money.

Avoiding Child Support

If the custodial parent does not ask for child support or take you to court, generally, you do not have to pay. But, if you fail to pay, the custodial parent may come back at a later date and ask for more money. The child support may be retroactive and you may be ordered to pay for the years you failed to pay.

Basically, there is no way to get out of paying child support. Few people come right out and ask the question of whether they can totally avoid paying child support, but it is one that is in the back of the minds of many. This question manifests itself in the way people behave—through purposefully suppressing income, concealing assets, or simply not paying. The repercussions for failing to pay child support include the following.

- *Contempt of Court.* A parent who violates a court order to pay child support can be held in contempt of court. The initial violation will usually result in a slap on the wrist and a stern warning from the judge.
- *Jail Sentence.* Willfully disobeying an order to pay child support can result in an active jail sentence and fine. The term of the sentence can extend until such time as the back child support is paid.
- *Wage Assignment Order.* A wage assignment order is an order from the court directing an employer to deduct the child support payment from the earnings of an employee and then make this payment directly to the person entitled to receive it as child support.
- *Garnishment.* Courts have the power to intercept the state and federal tax refunds of persons who owe back child support.
- *Revocation of Professional License.* There are a few states that allow holding a professional license for someone failing to pay child support.
- *Termination of Parental Rights.* A parent who has been ordered to pay child support and willfully fails to pay can be subject to having his or her parental rights terminated by the opposing parent.
- *Attachment or Levy.* If the person who owes child support has money in a bank or owns valuable property, the court can seize the assets and give them to the person who is entitled to receive child support.

PARENT TIP

If the custodial parent informs you that child support is not necessary, you should get a written statement from the parent to this effect. Otherwise, the custodial parent may later go to court, asking that you be ordered to pay child support going back to the day the child was conceived.

Manner of Payment

Child support payments are generally made in periodic payments on a weekly, biweekly, semimonthly, monthly, or quarterly basis, depending on your pay schedule. Generally, buying clothes, food, and other things children need in lieu of making actual child support payments will not be acceptable child support. The actual manner in which payments are made are made is through one of two ways.

1. *Direct Payments.* The parent ordered to pay child support can send payments directly to the parent entitled to receive it.

2. *Wage Withholding.* This can be initiated voluntarily by the parent obligated to pay child support or the court can order a wage Withholding. Once the agency that is responsible for collecting child support receives the funds, they will either send the parent entitled to the money a check or deposit the funds directly into his or her account.

Collecting Child Support

When a noncustodial parent has not paid all or part of the child support obligation that the court has ordered him or her to pay, he or she is considered to be in arrears. The unpaid amount plus interest accrues as an *arrearage*. Arrearages are considered to be unadjudicated until the court confirms the owed amount, then that amount is considered adjudicated arrearage, which means the custodial parent can take legal action to collect the payment. You will need an attorney to assist with the collection of the money to which you are entitled.

Misuse of Payments

You may go back to court if you suspect that the money you are paying in child support is not being used on behalf of the children. In most states, the person receiving child support has no duty to keep an accounting of how the money received as child support will be allocated on behalf of the children. If you file, it is not likely the judge will be able to do anything to change the situation. This is not an unusual allegation, and more often than not, it is without merit.

The judge may lecture the opposing parent about using the money for the child. If the children are being neglected and going without food or clothing, the noncustodial parent may need to contact the state or county child welfare agency. However, this should be done as a last resort and only when warranted, not as a form of retaliation or punishment.

Additional Financial Assistance

Generally, a parent's child support obligation is limited to whatever is included in the child support order. He or she does not legally have to pay any more than what the judge ordered. However, parents should allow their conscience to be their guide, keeping in mind that any such financial assistance will be considered a gift, and you will not be allowed to have it credited toward the child support obligation.

Termination of Child Support

You have to pay child support payments until the earlier of one of these events takes place:

- the child is emancipated;
- a court rules you are no longer capable of paying child support;
- the child dies;
- you die (however, your estate may still be held responsible);
- your parental rights are terminated;
- the child reaches the age of majority and is no longer attending high school;
- the child graduates from high school;
- the child becomes self-supporting; or,
- the termination condition ordered by the court in a previous child support order.

Keep in mind, however, that your child support obligation will not automatically go away. If you are under an order to pay, before you stop paying, you should file a motion to have your payments terminated. If you stop paying prior to that time, you may suffer serious consequences.

Modification of Child Support

The amount of child support you are ordered to pay is not engraved in stone. It can be modified by the court to reflect a significant change in circumstances. The following events may trigger a change in the amount of a child support award.

- ◆ A significant increase or decrease (usually 15%) in your income.
- ◆ An increase in the child's expenses. For example, the child support amount might be increased if the child needs braces or rehabilitation due to a car accident.
- ◆ You or the opposing parent has another child who you have the responsibility to support.

High and Low Incomes

You may not be stuck with whatever the guidelines determine is the appropriate child support award. There are instances when you can petition the court to deviate from the amount determined by the child support guidelines. Most judges will deviate from the guidelines when the parents have incomes that combine for more than a certain amount specified in the law (such as $150,000 per year), or incomes at or below the minimum-wage earning level.

Child Support and Visitation

There are many instances when a custodial parent will not allow the noncustodial parent to visit until child support is paid. There are also cases when a noncustodial parent will refuse to pay child support until he or she has visits with the child. Both parents in these situations are wrong. Child support is not a payment to see a child. Visitation is not a reward for paying child support. One really has nothing to do with the other.

If you are ordered to pay child support, you are obligated to pay regardless of whether you are ever allowed to see the child. If you are ordered to allow your child to visit with the other parent, you must do so even if you never receive a dime of child support. If you violate a court order, you risk being held in contempt and possibly jailed.

Child Support and Your Will

You do not have to provide for your children in your will. With respect to your children, you are free to divide your estate in any way you decide is appropriate. However, some states will require that minor children are given some support from your estate.

Bankruptcy

Bankruptcy protection does not affect a parent's obligation to pay child support. For example, if John owes Jane $8,000 in past due child support payments and he files a bankruptcy petition, the $8,000 will not be discharged by a bankruptcy action. However, if Jane is in the process of taking legal action to collect the $8,000, the bankruptcy action will temporarily prohibit Jane from pursuing collection action. The process of reinstating the collection action is fairly complicated and will require the assistance of an attorney who specializes in bankruptcies. While the bad news is that the bankruptcy will slow the collection process, the good news is that the bankruptcy will allow the opposing parent to reduce their other debt, which may make it easier for them to pay their child support payments.

Tax Implications

Generally, the parent who has primary physical custody of the minor child is entitled to claim the minor child as a deduction for state and federal income tax purposes. Sometimes parents agree to alternate turns claiming their minor child on their taxes. It is important to note that both parents cannot claim the child as a deduction. This practice can create serious tax consequences and is a violation of the tax rules.

EVALUATING YOUR SITUATION

There are basically three things you need to know in order to calculate child support:

1. your income;
2. the other parent's income; and,
3. your state's child support guidelines.

PARENT TIP

In most cases, there will not be much room for argument about child support. The child support guidelines or formula will be applied to the incomes of you and the other parent, and the child support amount is determined mathematically. The only places for argument will be whether you or the other parent accurately reported income, and whether your child has any special needs that require additional child support.

From your pay stubs for this year, and from last year's W-2 form and income tax return, you should know your gross income. If you are the custodial parent, you will also have a good idea of the cost of health insurance, day care, and other special needs of your child. Unless you happen to know what the other parent earns, you will just have to estimate what he or she earns. (Refer to the section in this chapter on "How Child Support is Determined," as well as your state's support guidelines, for more information on what constitutes income, how net income is determined, etc.)

Once you determine the income for you and the other parent, you need to plug that information into your state's child support guidelines or formula to get an estimate of how much child support is likely to be ordered. Because each state's child support guidelines are different, it is impossible to be more specific here. (See the listing for your state in Appendix A for information about where to find your state's child support guidelines.)

Seeking Child Support

If a child support order is being sought for the first time, the incomes of the parties and the child support guidelines will determine the amount of child support to be paid.

Changing Child Support

In order to increase or decrease child support, the person seeking the change will need to show that financial circumstances have changed since the current child support order was issued. In most cases, this will mean showing that there has been a significant change in the income of at least one of the parents. If you want an increase in child support, you will need to show that the other parent's income has increased, or that your income has decreased. If you want a decrease in child support, you will need to show that your income has decreased, or the other parent's income has increased. If the current order was above the regular child support schedule because your child had special needs, a change in those special needs could also be a basis for a change in child support.

Enforcing Child Support

All states have a state agency designated to enforce child support orders on behalf of custodial parents who receive AFDC benefits. Usually, the collection services of that agency is also available to other custodial parents who request services.

Locating absent parents. The whereabouts of the noncustodial parent must be known to enforce a child support order. Locating the noncustodial parent can be a lengthy process if the noncustodial parent is not employed. You can try to locate the parent through his or her Social Security number and date of birth. You can also use credit bureaus and the Internet to search for the noncustodial parent.

Information required. To help your attorney or child support office locate an absent parent, you must provide the following information (if known) to your caseworker.

- ◆ The absent parent's Social Security number. You may be able to find this by reviewing old pay stubs, income tax returns, loan applications, checking or savings accounts, health insurance records, or military records.
- ◆ The absent parent's address.
- ◆ The absent parent's date of birth.
- ◆ The absent parent's employer's name and phone number.
- ◆ A photograph or physical description of the absent parent.
- ◆ The names of friends and relatives of the noncustodial parent and organizations to which he or she may belong.

Defending a Child Support Claim

If you are being sued, there is little you can do to completely avoid child support. If you do not believe the child is yours, you can dispute paternity. This will usually lead to a paternity action being filed against you. (see Chapter 7.) The only other way you might avoid a child support order is if you are receiving some type of welfare benefits as your only source of income. See the section of this chapter on "How Child Support is Determined" for more information on what type of benefits do and do not constitute income for child support purposes.

In most cases, what you will be arguing about is the *amount* of child support. There are only three things that can be argued here:
1. your income is actually less than stated by the other parent or in a report from an investigator;
2. the other parent's income is actually more than stated by the other parent or in a report from an investigator; or,
3. the child's special needs are less than stated by the other parent or in a report from an investigator.

In a case involving a request to raise or lower child support, you can also argue either that there has been no change since the last order was issued, or that the change in income or needs is so small that it does not merit a change in the child support amount.

PREPARING AND FILING LEGAL FORMS

The parties in child support disputes will generally include the custodial parent (or whoever has custody of the child) and the noncustodial parent.

Child Support Complaint

The following information should be included in the *Child Support Complaint:*
- the state statute that covers child support actions (look for "Child Support" in the index to your state statute);
- the length of time you have resided in the state and the name of the county where you are a resident;

- the length of time the other party has resided in the state and the name of the county he or she is a resident;
- your relationship to the minor child;
- the child's name and their date of birth;
- a statement regarding the defendant's relationship to the minor child;
- a statement regarding when and how you obtained custody of the minor child;
- a statement that the defendant is able-bodied, employed, and capable of providing child support;
- a statement that the child is in need of support; and,
- a statement regarding whether the child has any extraordinary expenses.

Summons

If you are seeking an initial child support order, you will need to prepare and file a *Summons* along with your *Child Support Complaint*. See Chapter 5 for information about the Summons.

Supporting Documents

In addition to some type of cover sheet, the most common supporting document in a child support case is the *Financial Affidavit*. Many states have their own form, so be sure to check with the court clerk. This type of form has different names in different states, such as *Financial Statement*, *Financial Affidavit*, or *Statement of Net Worth*.

Filing with the Court Clerk

After you have prepared all of the documents that are required to begin your case, you will need to file them with the court clerk. See Chapter 5 for more information about filing with the court clerk.

NOTIFYING NECESSARY PARTIES

Whether you are seeking to establish child support, or seeking to increase or decrease child support, you will need to notify the other parent. If you are seeking a decrease and the other parent is receiving

AFDC benefits for the child, you may also need to notify the state social service agency managing the AFDC program.

THE HEARING
For more information on how to schedule a court hearing, see the section on "Scheduling Court Hearings" in Chapter 6.

Notifying Necessary Parties
The parties you will need to notify are those who were notified when you filed your request to establish or change child support, as well as any witnesses you intend to have testify. In child support cases, the most common witnesses are employers, or other third parties who can verify the income of the other parent. For more information on notifying parties of court hearings, see the section on "Notifying Necessary Parties" in Chapter 5. For more information about notifying witnesses, see the section on "Witnesses" in Chapter 6.

Preparing for the Hearing
See Chapter 6 for more information about preparing for your hearing. In a child support case, the primary emphasis will be on the accuracy of the income information of you and the other party. In some cases, you may also need to establish the special needs of a child.

Presenting Your Case
For more information, see the section on "Presenting Your Case" in Chapter 6.

The Judgment
After the judge announces his or her decision, you will need to prepare an order for the judge to sign. For more information, see the section on "The Judge's Decision and Final Order" in Chapter 6.

-11-
TERMINATION OF PARENTAL RIGHTS

Termination of parental rights is a court action that severs all legal ties between the parent and the child, and is considered to be one of the most severe court actions that can be brought against a parent. Once parental rights are terminated, there is no way to revive the legal ties between a parent and child (except through an adoption). However, it is highly unlikely that a court would approve an adoption by a parent whose parental rights were terminated.

TERMINATION OF PARENTAL RIGHTS LAW AND PROCEDURE

Although the results are severe, proceedings for termination of parental rights are fairly common in the following situations:

- in adoption proceedings when the biological parent will not consent to the adoption or cannot be located or
- in cases of severe abuse or neglect, when the child protection agency believes the chances of reuniting the child and the parents are so hopeless that the child should be placed for adoption.

Termination of parental rights actions gained a lot of notoriety in the case of Gregory K. He was the young man who hired a lawyer to terminate his parents' rights so his foster family could adopt him. The state law would not allow the foster parents to bring an action, so Gregory K. had to bring an action on his own behalf.

Another highly publicized termination of parental rights case was the one in which two babies were switched at birth. When one of the children became ill and died, the parents discovered the child did not belong to them. They went in search of their child, and when they found her, she did not want to be reunited with them. The child filed papers to have her biological parents' rights terminated so that she could remain with the family that had raised her.

Termination of parental rights is a civil proceeding. Generally, the proceeding is held in *closed session*, which means, unlike most cases, the general public will not be allowed to sit in on the hearings. A closed session is considered necessary in termination of parental rights cases because the facts are sensitive and it is necessary to protect the privacy and identity of the children.

Because the consequences of a termination proceeding are severe, the court can appoint an attorney to represent the person whose rights are subject to being terminated in the proceeding. The person initiating the termination proceeding must prove the case with *clear and convincing evidence*. This standard of proof is higher than the traditional standard in civil cases (called a *preponderance of the evidence*), because state legislatures want to make it difficult to terminate parents' rights. Generally, the termination proceeding will be presided over by a judge, not a jury.

You can appeal the judge's decision. However, unless the judge clearly abuses his or her discretion, it is not likely that the appeal will be successful.

Who Can Seek Termination of Parental Rights

The following people and organizations can terminate the parental rights action.

  ◆ *The state or county child welfare agency.* These agencies are responsible for initiating the majority of termination of parental rights proceedings—it is their responsibility to protect children. The child welfare agency is likely to have the information and evidence that will support a finding that a parent's rights should be terminated. The agency moves to terminate parental rights in cases when it is believed that such action will protect the child.

  ◆ *A custodial parent.* The parent who has been caring for the child can move to have the other parent's rights terminated.

- *A guardian ad litem.* This is someone who has been appointed by the court to represent the child's best interest and to act on the child's behalf. In most jurisdictions, children are not prohibited from initiating termination of parental rights actions. However, children usually do so through the appointment of a guardian ad litem or by having some adult acting on their behalf.
- *A person seeking to adopt the child.*
- *Grandparents or other members of the child's extended family.*
- *A person with knowledge of the fact alleged in the Complaint seeking to terminate the parent's rights.*
- *Any **interested person** or a person with a **legitimate interest** in the child's well-being.*

Most states do not allow foster parents to move to terminate the rights of the child's parents. Children are placed in foster care while their parents get their act together. It is believed parents will resist getting help if they believe they could lose custody to a foster parent.

PARENT TIP

Child welfare agencies will usually work to help parents learn to properly care for their child before they will move for a termination of parental rights. It is the states' interest to restore families and keep children with their parents.

Effect on the Other Parent

Terminating the rights of one parent has no impact on the other parent's rights, unless both parents were parties in the termination proceeding. The facts might exist to justify terminating the rights of one parent, but not the rights of the other.

Grounds for Terminating Parental Rights

Each state legislature designates a set of grounds that will support a request to terminate a parent's rights. Generally, the law will only require that one of the grounds be established or proven. However, it is always a good idea to establish as many of the grounds on the list as possible. Sometimes the cumulative effect of the evidence can go a

PARENT TIP

State law requires that certain *grounds* or circumstances exist before a person can seek to have a parent's rights terminated. A child that is not happy with the rules his or her parents impose cannot move to have his or her parents rights' terminated. A parent who does not wish to pay child support would not be able to have his or her parental rights terminated.

long way in establishing that a parent's rights should be terminated. The following are some of the more common grounds for termination of parental rights.

Abandonment. The general rule is that a parent who abandons his or her child for six months or longer is subject to having their parental rights terminated.

Abandonment can come in two forms. The first is called *physical abandonment*. An example might be a situation in which a couple breaks up and the children are placed in the custody of the mother. The father is awarded visitation, and after a few months, the father stops visiting and simply drops out of the picture. He does not call, make visitation arrangements, or send any child support payments.

The other form of abandonment is referred to as *constructive abandonment*. One court explained it as what takes place when "a parent withholds his presence, his love, his care, the opportunity to display filial affection and willfully neglects to lend support and maintenance." Even if you are physically present but do not perform the function of a parent, you could be held to have constructively abandoned your child.

Constructive abandonment is a form of neglect. For this reason, a parent who has a child in foster care and fails to follow through on the steps needed to have the child returned to him or her might be considered to have abandoned the child.

One of the key components of both forms of abandonment is that the conduct of the parent must be *willful*. There must be some proof that the reason the parent is not physically or emotionally present for his or her children is because he or she *chooses* not to be. For example, it is not abandonment if a parent is not aware of where their child lives because the opposing parent has concealed his or her whereabouts, or if limited resources keep him or her from supporting or visiting. If a parent is doing the best he or she can under the circumstances, it is not likely he or she will be found to have abandoned a child.

Failing to acknowledge paternity. Failing to acknowledge paternity within six months after the child's birth might be grounds for terminating parental rights. However, before a man's rights can be terminated on this basis, it must be shown that he knew or had reason to know that he was the father of the child.

Incarceration. In some states, a parent's incarceration is grounds for the termination of parental rights. However, in most jurisdictions, just being incarcerated is not enough. The courts consider three factors in determining whether the parent's incarceration should be enough to support the termination of parental rights.

1. *What was the situation before the parent was incarcerated?* If the parent did not pay child support or only did so sporadically, and visited infrequently prior to the incarceration, it is more likely the incarceration will be deemed abandonment and a judge will be inclined to terminate the parental rights. However, if the parent was a consistent and positive presence in the child's life prior to going to jail, it is not likely the court will terminate that parent's rights on the basis of incarceration.

2. *How willing is the parent to rehabilitate and behave in a way that reflects concern about the child's best interest?* If there is a situation in which a parent has an isolated incident of incarceration, gets out of jail, and behaves properly, it is not likely that the parental rights will be terminated on the basis of the incarceration. However, if the parent is a career criminal and repeat offender and does not show any inclination or interest in becoming a law-abiding citizen, the court is more likely to terminate the parental rights.

3. *How long is the sentence the parent received?* The longer the sentence the parent received, the more likely the court will ter-

minate the parental rights. If a life sentence without the possibility of parole was received, it is difficult to imagine how a
parent will be deemed not to have abandoned his or her child.
However, a sentence of shorter duration might not be enough
to support a finding of termination of parental rights.

Mental incapacity. Mental incapacity can come in the form of
mental illness or mental retardation, and must exist to the extent
that it renders the parent unable to care for the child. Most states
do not require the person to have been determined incompetent
by a court of law or to have a condition that is universally recognized in the psychiatric community. In termination proceedings,
courts focus on the parent's ability to care for the children. There
is usually a requirement that the mental incapacity be a permanent condition or one that is not likely to be cured or corrected
in the immediate future.

Establishing mental incapacity will ordinarily require the expert
testimony of a psychiatrist or psychologist. The testimony of a social
worker or the opposing parent alone will not be sufficient.

Neglect. Neglect allegations focus more on the condition of the
children than any specific conduct of the parent. For example, a
parent's addiction to drugs alone is not enough to terminate
parental rights. However, when the addiction negatively impacts
the ability to care for the children, it becomes neglect and can result
in the termination of parental rights.

Almost every petition to terminate parental rights will
include neglect allegations. Neglect has been used to support a
finding that parental rights should be terminated based on the
following allegations.

- ◆ A parent failed to provide child support required by a court
  order. Parents are expected to use the financial resources at
  their disposal to support their children.
- ◆ A parent allowed young children to stay at home alone for several hours at night while he or she went out with friends.

◆ A parent failed to provide children with food and appropriate clothing, routinely sending the child to school without a coat during the winter months and without lunch money, for example.

◆ A parent failed to protect the children from abuse inflicted by the other parent.

Abuse. Physical and sexual abuse both are grounds for the termination of parental rights. In many jurisdictions, an isolated instance of abuse, if sufficiently extreme, can support a finding that a parent's rights should be terminated.

Because of the severity of these allegations, courts usually will intervene more rapidly to protect the children from future danger. This is especially true with testimony that the parent is not likely to benefit or has not benefited from counseling, or has failed to take steps to minimize future abuse.

Defenses

The best way to defend against a termination of parental rights action is to show the court that terminating parental rights will have an adverse impact on the child. Provide evidence of a loving relationship between parent and child, despite whatever evidence there may be to the contrary. For example, a parent who has not paid child support could still argue that he or she has visited regularly and has a positive influence on the child.

A parent whose rights are subject to termination might show that there has been a significant change since the Complaint or petition was filed. For example, a parent could show evidence of drug rehabilitation or corrected whatever problems existed prior to and at the time the petition was filed. It would be a good idea to have testimony from experts to corroborate the change and testify to the unlikeliness of reoccurring behavior.

The best defense to a termination of parental rights action may be a clean suit and a sob story. Courts are reluctant to terminate parental rights and are generally looking for reasons not to terminate. If you can convince the judge of your love and future commitment to caring for the child, you are likely to be able to convince him or her not to terminate your rights.

The Court Decision

The judge who presides over a termination of parental rights proceeding must find two things:

1. the person who filed the petition has established the grounds cited in the statute (see Appendix A) and
2. terminating parental rights will be in the child's best interest.

If both of these elements are not present, the judge has no authority to terminate the parent's rights. Courts are given discretion, but even if they feel terminating would be in a child's best interest they cannot terminate the parent's rights unless at least one of the grounds is proven. Similarly, if termination is not in the child's best interest, the judge cannot terminate even if the grounds exist.

Courts are more likely to terminate the parental rights of a parent in situations when someone is waiting to adopt the child, whether it is a stepparent adoption or a private adoption. The court does not want to leave children without a parent or to condemn them to a life in the foster care system.

Once the final order terminating parental rights is entered, it ends the parent's obligation to pay child support and extinguishes the right to visit or have a relationship with the child. The terminated parent's consent will no longer be needed for adoption. It also terminates the parent's right to inherit from the child. However, in most jurisdictions the child will continue to be entitled to inherit from the parent even after their parental rights are terminated until the child is adopted or reaches the age of majority.

PREPARING AND FILING LEGAL FORMS

The following are examples of why a parent might file a termination of parental rights action against the other parent.

♦ He or she does not want the parent who has abandoned the child for several years to show up and disrupt the child's life.

- ◆ He or she is ill and wants to ensure that if something happens to him or her, the child will go to someone other than the other parent.
- ◆ He or she wants the child to be adopted by a stepparent.
- ◆ The child is wealthy and the filing parent does not want the parent who has abandoned the child to have access to the child's assets.

The Parties
The parties in a *Petition to Terminate Parental Rights* will usually line up in one of the following ways.
- ◆ *Custodial Parent v. Noncustodial Parent*
- ◆ *Prospective Adoptive Parent v. Noncustodial Parent*
- ◆ *Child Welfare Agency v. Parents*

Petition to Terminate Parental Rights
The following information should be included in the *Petition to Terminate Parental Rights:*
- ◆ the name of the state statute that governs termination of parental rights actions (look for "Termination of Parental Rights" in the appendix to your state statute);
- ◆ the name of the minor child who is the subject of the petition and his or her date of birth;
- ◆ the respondent's relationship to minor child;
- ◆ the state where the respondent resides and how long he or she is believed to have resided there;
- ◆ the petitioner's relationship to the minor child;
- ◆ the state where the petitioner resides and how long they are believed to reside there prior to the filing of the petition;
- ◆ the relationship between petitioner and respondent, if any;
- ◆ a statement regarding whether anyone has been appointed as guardian ad litem for the child in this or any other action;
- ◆ the reasons the respondent's rights are subject to being terminated (refer to Appendix A); and,
- ◆ a statement that the petition has not been filed to circumvent the provisions of the Uniform Child Custody Jurisdiction Act.

Summons

You will need to prepare and file a *Summons* along with your *Petition to Terminate Parental Rights*. See Chapter 5 for information about the Summons.

Supporting Documents

Other than some type of cover sheet, there are not usually any supporting documents filed with a *Petition to Terminate Parental Rights*.

Filing with the Court Clerk

After you have prepared all of the documents that are required to begin your case, you will need to file them with the court clerk. See Chapter 5 for more information about filing with the court clerk.

NOTIFYING NECESSARY PARTIES

In all cases you will need to notify the other parent. If the other parent cannot be located, you will probably need to publish a notice in a newspaper. (see Chapter 5.) Of all of the various types of legal proceedings involving parents, the termination of parental rights is probably the most serious. Therefore, it is absolutely essential to properly notify all of the necessary parties.

THE HEARING

As with any court hearing, there are certain steps you must follow, as well as ways to be more thoroughly prepared for the experience.

Scheduling a Hearing

For more information on how to schedule a court hearing, see the section on "Scheduling Court Hearings" in Chapter 6.

Notifying Necessary Parties

The parties you will need to notify are those who were notified when you filed your *Petition to Terminate Parental Rights*, as well as any witnesses you intend to have testify. For more information about notifying parties, see the section on "Notifying Necessary Parties" in

Chapter 5. For more information about notifying witnesses, see the section on "Witnesses" in Chapter 6.

Preparing for the Hearing

See Chapter 6 for more information about preparing for your hearing. In a termination of parental rights case, the primary emphasis will be on proving one or more of the grounds listed in your state's laws that justify termination.

Presenting Your Case

For more information about how to present your case, see the section on "Presenting Your Case" in Chapter 6.

The Judgment

After the judge announces his or her decision, you will need to prepare an order for the judge to sign. For more information, see the section on "The Judge's Decision and Final Order" in Chapter 6.

GLOSSARY

A

abandonment. The withholding of contact, love, or financial support from a minor child. Abandonment is grounds for the termination of parental rights. Before a court will terminate a parent's rights on these grounds, there must be a showing that his or her conduct is willful or intentional. A father cannot be found to have abandoned a child that he did not know existed.

abuse. Any conduct by a parent that endangers the physical and emotional well-being and development of his or her child. Abuse can take many forms, including physical assault, verbal attacks, or inappropriate sexual contact. A single instance of abuse, depending on its severity, can be grounds for terminating parental rights.

adoption. Court action that results in the creation of a parent-child relationship where it did not previously exist. A minor child cannot be adopted unless his or her parents give their consent, are deceased, or their rights are terminated. An adoptive parent has the same rights and responsibilities as a biological parent.

Aid to Families with Dependent Children (AFDC). A form of welfare benefits. Generally, if a custodial parent is receiving AFDC, the appropriate state agency will pursue the noncustodial parent to pay child support and possibly reimburse the government for the payments made on behalf of the minor child.

arrears. Unpaid child support payments. A parent who falls too far behind in child support payments is subject to having his or her paycheck and income tax return garnished, and may face imprisonment.

automatic paternity. Paternity that is presumed as a consequence of the relationship of the parties. A man does not have to submit to a test to establish paternity of a child his wife conceived during their marriage.

B

best interest of the child. Often referred to as the *polar star*, it is the compass judges follow when making decisions regarding custody, visitation, and termination of parental rights.

biological parents. The two people responsible for conceiving a child. Also referred to as *birth parents* or *natural parents*.

birth parents. *See biological parents.*

C

change of circumstances. In most jurisdictions, a court must find that there has been a significant change of circumstances before it will modify an existing custody order. Generally, the change of circumstances must relate to a condition or situation in the custodial home that adversely impacts the best interest of the child.

child support. The amount of money a noncustodial parent is obligated to pay on behalf of his or her minor child(ren).

child support guidelines. A mathematical formula that is created by a state's legislature and used to determine a noncustodial parents child support obligation.

civil contempt. When a party fails to do what the court ordered him or her to do. Civil contempt is punishable by fine and imprisonment.

clear and convincing evidence. The standard of proof in termination of parental rights cases. Before an opposing party can succeed in terminating a parent's parental rights, he or she must establish by clear and convincing evidence that there are grounds to do so.

codes. *See statutes.*

complainant. The party who initiates or originally files the court action.

complaint. The document the complainant or petitioner files to begin the legal process. It identifies the nature of the proceeding and outlines facts to support the complainant's request that the case be decided in his or her favor.

constructive abandonment. A parent who has regular contact with his or her minor child, yet willfully and intentionally refuses to consistently fulfill his or her duties and responsibilities as a parent, could be held to have constructively abandoned his or her child. Constructive abandonment is a form of neglect.

custodial parent. Generally refers to the parent who either by consent or court order has custody of the minor child.

custody. Refers to the control or authority exercised by a parent over his or her minor child.

D

defendant. The person who is being sued.

diligent search. Before a party can be served with a complaint by publishing a notice in a newspaper, the plaintiff must engage in a diligent search for his or her whereabouts.

divided custody. A custody arrangement in which both parents have primary physical custody of at least one of the children and the parents do not share custody of any of the children.

DNA testing.   The most common paternity test, which uses DNA or genetic traits to determine whether a given man could be the biological father of a given child.

E

emancipation.   A court action in which a parent's rights or authority is relinquished. Minor children who are married, enlisted in the military, or self-supporting can petition the court to be emancipated.

expert witness.   A witness who has a special knowledge of the subject about which he or she is to testify. Psychiatrists and child psychologists are examples of expert witnesses.

extraordinary expenses.   Expenses incurred by a minor child that are not usual or customary. These expenses are taken into account when calculating child support. The court determines whether or not an expense is extraordinary.

F

financial affidavit.   A sworn statement, which includes information about the party's income, expenses, what they own, and debt. The information is used to calculate child support and to satisfy the court that the party seeking custody is able to support the minor child.

G

genetic sampling.   *See DNA testing.*

gross income.   A party's income before any taxes or other items are deducted. Gross income is used to calculate a noncustodial parents child support obligation.

guardian ad litem.   A person appointed by the court to advocate on behalf of the best interests of the minor child in a termination of parental rights action.

H

hearsay rule. A rule that prohibits a witness from testifying about statements made by someone who is not a party to the proceeding. The hearsay rule is designed to ensure the integrity of the testimony presented in court.

home studies. A report prepared by social workers after visiting the parties' homes and observing how the child interacts with each parent. The report is used by the court to make a custody determination. Home studies are also used in adoption cases.

I

imputed income. It is the income a parent has the potential to receive if he or she were to obtain employment in a field that is compatible with his or her education, training, experience, or background.

income. The amount of money a person receives from the following sources: salaries, wages, commissions, bonuses, dividends, severance pay, pensions, interest, annuities, capital gains, Social Security, workers' compensation, unemployment insurance, disability pay, gifts, or prizes.

interested person. A person with a legitimate interest in a minor child's well-being, and therefore has standing to initiate a custody or termination of parental rights action against a natural parent(s).

J

joint custody. A situation in which both parents share responsibility for decision making and physical custody of a minor child.

joint managing conservatorship. In some states, such as Texas, it is the phrase used to describe a joint custody arrangement.

L

legal custody. A parent who has the authority to make decisions on behalf of his or her minor child regarding matters such as medical treatment, education, and religious training is deemed to have legal custody. It is not unusual for a court to award one parent sole physical custody and allow both parents to have joint legal custody.

legal guardian. An officer or agent of the court who is appointed to protect the interests of minor children and to provide for their care, welfare, education, maintenance, and support.

M

material change of circumstances. *See significant change of circumstances.*

maternal preference. A preference some judges have to keep children in their tender years with their mother. This is not the law in most states.

mediation. An intervention, ordered by the court in custody disputes, to promote reconciliation, settlement, and compromise between the parties. In many states, mediation is mandatory. In these jurisdictions, the judge cannot hear a case until after the party's have participated in mediation.

minor child. A child who has not yet reached the age of majority. The age of majority in most states is 18 years old.

motion. A document that is filed with the court when the parties already have an open case. Motions follow the same format as a petition or complaint. A party files a motion to ask the court to order the opposing party to take or refrain from a specific action.

N

natural parents. *See biological parents.*

neglect. The failure and willful indifference of a parent in the fulfillment of his or her duties and responsibilities for the care and maintenance of his or her minor child. Neglect is grounds for termination of parental rights.

noncustodial parent. A parent who does not share a residence with his or her minor child.

P

parens patriae. A Latin term that relates to the concept of divorce courts acting on behalf of the state to protect and control the property and custody of minor children.

parental liability. The responsibility a parent has for the torts or the wrongful acts committed by his or her minor children. Most states have laws that limit the dollar amount of a parent's liability.

parenting plan. A plan created by parents' that outlines the custody arrangement they feel is in their minor child's best interest. The plan is filed with the court and used by the judge in making custody determinations.

paternity. The state of being a father.

paternity action. A civil lawsuit that a person files to ask a court to determine whether a given man could be the biological father of a given child.

paternity affidavit. A written statement signed before a notary or other official, in which the father acknowledges paternity. The affidavit must also be signed by the mother.

petition. *See complaint.*

petitioner. *See complainant.*

physical abandonment. A parent who chooses not to have physical contact and to separate him- or herself from his or her minor child for an extended period of time (usually six months or longer) is deemed to have physically abandoned the child. In most states, incarceration is not considered to be the equivalent of physical abandonment.

physical custody. In a custody arrangement, the parent with whom a minor child resides is deemed to have physical custody.

physical placement. The term some states use to describe where a minor child resides.

plaintiff. *See complainant.*

preponderance of the evidence. The traditional standard of proof in civil cases. In a custody case, for example, the party whose evidence is more convincing will prevail.

primary caretaker. The parent who provides for the minor child's day-to-day care. The primary caretaker often has an advantage in custody disputes.

primary custody. In joint custody arrangements, the parent with whom the child resides for the majority of days each year is said to have primary custody.

putative father. The man alleged to have fathered the child whose parent status is at issue in a paternity suit.

R

relevancy. The facts and evidence a party presents at trial must relate to the case at hand. Evidence will be deemed relevant if it has a tendency to prove a fact in issue.

respondent. *See defendant.*

S

secondary custody. In joint custody arrangements, the parent with whom the child does not spend the majority of days each year is said to have secondary custody. A parent who has been awarded visitation might also be deemed to have secondary custody.

shared custody. *See joint custody.*

shared parental responsibility. The term some states use to describe joint custody.

sole custody. The term used to describe situations in which one parent is awarded both physical and legal custody.

standing. The law only allows certain people to initiate lawsuits. Such persons are said to have standing. State statutes outline who is allowed or has standing to file paternity, custody, visitation, or child support actions.

statutes. The set of volumes that contain the laws passed by a state's legislature. Also referred to as *codes*.

summons. A form, usually available from the clerk of court, that must be delivered to the person being sued. The Summons, which is attached to the Complaint, puts the defendant on notice that he or she must file some kind of response to the Complaint within a certain number of days, and that if a response is not filed, he or she may lose the case by default.

supervised visitation. Visitation that must take place under the direct supervision of someone selected by the court. Such supervision is ordered by the court based on the judge's conclusion that the visiting parent poses a threat to the child if not supervised.

status quo. The condition or situation that existed at the time a court action is commenced. In custody disputes, courts are reluctant to disrupt the status quo or remove a minor child from a place where he or she is thriving and developing normally.

T

termination of parental rights. A court action that severs all legal ties between the parent and the minor child. It is considered to be one of the most severe court actions that can be brought against a parent.

third-party custody. When the court awards custody of a minor child to someone other than a natural parent, for example, a grandparent.

third-party visitation. Visitation with a minor child awarded to someone other than the noncustodial parent, for example, a grandparent.

U

unfit parent. A parent who is incompetent or unsuitable to have the care or control of his or her minor child(ren). Unfitness generally relates to some type of moral delinquency.

Uniform Child Custody Jurisdiction Act (UCCJA). A law that dictates that a court cannot enter or modify a court order until the minor child has resided in the state for at least six months, and the court is made aware of any prior or pending custody disputes and the name of any person who is not a party to the legal action, but has a legal claim to the minor child.

Uniform Child Custody Jurisdiction Affidavit. The affidavit containing the information required by the UCCJA. It must be attached to all custody and visitation complaints.

Uniform Interstate Family Support Act. A federal law that requires states to cooperate in the collection of child support. It ensures there is only one valid support order to enforce when more than one state is involved in a case.

V

verification. A sworn statement in which a party declares that all of the information included in the complaint is true, because he or she either knows first hand or believes it to be true.

visitation. The opportunity the court grants to noncustodial parents to visit with a minor child on a prescribed schedule.

W

witness. A person who testifies in a court proceeding.

APPENDIX A:
STATE-BY-STATE LAWS

This appendix contains an alphabetical listing of the fifty states and the District of Columbia. Each state's listing includes basic information that should assist you in preparing your legal forms and finding any additional information you may need. (The abbreviation "Sec." means section.)

The Law   This listing provides the name of the set of books that contain the state's laws, and an example of how they are divided into sections, chapters, articles, etc. For example, under the listing for Alabama, you find the following notation:

Code of Alabama.
Example: Code of Alabama, Title 30, Chapter 2, Section 30-2-1 (C.A. Sec. 30-2-1).

This tells you that "Code of Alabama" is the title of the books containing the laws of Alabama. It also tells you that the books are subdivided into titles, chapters, and sections. "Code of Alabama, Title 30, Chapter 2, Section 30-2-1" is abbreviated "C.A. Sec. 30-2-1." You will often find that the section number incorporates the number of the title, chapter, article, etc. Ask the librarian to assist you in locating the volume that contains the laws governing the kind of case in which you are involved.

Case Style

This provides an example of the heading that should be placed at the beginning of any legal forms you file. You should verify the accuracy of the case style by reviewing a case file at the courthouse. If the case style used in the case file is different from the example included in this appendix, use the format your find in the case file at your local courthouse.

Designation of Parties

This tells you how you and the opposing party should be designated in court papers. This will either be *Plaintiff* and *Defendant,* or *Petitioner* and *Respondent.*

Custody

This provides a general summary of the factors a court will consider in determining custody.

Child Support

This provides a general summary of the state's child support laws. If your state has child support guidelines, contact the court clerk's office at the courthouse about where you can obtain a copy. They usually include instructions on how to use the guidelines. This section also indicates the age at which the child support obligation normally ends. (However, keep in mind that there may be extenuating factors that may extend a parent's obligation beyond the age cited in this listing.)

Termination of Parental Rights

This provides a general summary of the state's grounds for the termination of parental rights.

Alabama

The Law	Code of Alabama. ***Example:*** Code of Alabama, Title 30, Chapter 2, Section 30-2-1 (C.A. Sec. 30-2-1).
Case Style	IN THE CIRCUIT COURT FOR _____COUNTY, ALABAMA
Designation of Parties	_____, Plaintiff, and _____, Defendant.
Custody	Factors: (1) moral character of parents and (2) age and sex of child. Joint custody possible.
Child Support	Either parent may be ordered to pay, "as may seem right and proper, having regard to the moral character and prudence of the parents and age and sex of children." Termination age: 19.
Termination of Parental Rights	Grounds: (1) abandonment; (2) emotional or mental illness or mental deficiency of parent; (3) excessive substance abuse by parent; (4) child abused or in danger of abuse by parent; (5) physical injury of child resulting from neglect; and, (6) parent convicted and imprisoned for a felony.

Alaska

The Law

Alaska Statutes.
Example: Alaska Statutes, Title 25, Section 25.24.010 (A.S. Sec. 25.24.010).

Case Style

SUPERIOR COURT FOR THE STATE OF ALASKA # _____
JUDICIAL DISTRICT

Designation
of Parties

_____, Petitioner, vs.
_____, Respondent.

Custody

Factors: Best interest of the child considering: (1) physical, emotional, mental, religious, and social needs of the child; (2) capability and desire of each party to meet those needs; (3) child's preference, if of suitable age and ability; (4) love and affection existing between each child and each party; (5) length of time the child has been in a stable, satisfactory environment, and the desirability of maintaining continuity; (6) desire and ability of each party to allow an open, loving, and frequent relationship between the child and the other party; (7) any evidence of domestic violence, child abuse or neglect in the proposed custodial home, or history of violence between the parties; (8) any evidence that substance abuse by either party or other household member directly affects the child's emotional or physical well-being; and, (9) any other relevant factor.

Child Support	Factors: (1) child's needs; (2) ability of both parties to meet those needs; (3) extent of support by the parent during the marriage; and, (4) economic ability of each party to pay. Termination age: 18.
Termination of Parental Rights	Grounds: (1) parent without custody unreasonably withholds consent to adoption and (2) child was conceived as a result of sexual abuse of a minor.

Arizona

The Law	Arizona Revised Statutes. ***Example:*** Arizona Revised Statutes, Section 25-311 (A.R.S. Sec. 25-311).
Case Style	IN THE SUPERIOR COURT OF THE STATE OF ARIZONA IN AND FOR THE COUNTY OF _____
Designation of Parties	_____, Petitioner, and _____, Respondent.
Custody	Factors: Best interest of the child considering: (1) parties' wishes; (2) child's wishes; (3) interaction and interrelationship between the child and each parent, siblings and other significant persons; (4) child's adjustment to home, school, and community; (5) mental and physical health of all persons involved; (6) which parent is more likely to allow frequent and continuing contact with the other parent; (7) whether any parent provided primary care; (8) whether there was any coercion or duress by one parent in obtaining a custody agreement; and, (9) whether there was any domestic violence. Joint custody may be granted if the parties agree and submit a written joint custody agreement.

Child Support

State child support guidelines available from court clerk. Termination age: 18.

Termination of
Parental Rights

Grounds: (1) abandonment; (2) neglect or willful abuse of the child; (3) mental illness or mental deficiency of parent or chronic substance abuse by parent; (4) parent convicted and incarcerated for a felony of such as to prove parent unfit; (5) potential father failed to file paternity action within thirty days as prescribed by law; and, (6) parents relinquished rights to child to an agency or consented to adoption.

Arkansas

The Law	Arkansas Code of 1987 Annotated. **Example:** Arkansas Code Annotated, Title 9, Chapter 12, Section 9-12-301 (A.C.A. Sec. 9-12-301).
Case Style	IN THE CHANCERY COURT OF _____ ARKANSAS
Designation of Parties	_____, Plaintiff, vs. _____, Defendant.
Custody	Only statutory provision is that custody be determined "without regard to the sex of the parent but solely in accordance with the welfare and best interest of the child."
Child Support	Arkansas Family Support guidelines chart is available from Chancery Court Clerk. Termination age: 18.
Termination of Parental Rights	Grounds: 1) abandonment; (2) neglect or abuse; and, (3) parent without custody unreasonably withholds consent to adoption.

California

The Law	West's Annotated California Codes. **Example:** Family Code, Section 2300. (California has several Annotated California Codes, such as the Family Code, Probate Code, etc. Ask the librarian if you need assistance.)
Case Style	SUPERIOR COURT OF CALIFORNIA, COUNTY OF _____
Designation of Parties	_____, Petitioner, vs. _____, Respondent.
Custody	Factors: (1) child's health, safety, and welfare; (2) any history of abuse; (3) nature and amount of contact with each parent; and, (4) any other factor the court considers relevant. Marital misconduct may be considered.
Child Support	State child support guidelines available from court clerk. Termination age: 18.
Termination of Parental Rights	Grounds: (1) abandonment; (2) neglect or abuse of the child; (3) substance abuse by parent; (4) parent convicted of a felony; (5) emotional or mental illness or mental deficiency of parent; and, (6) out of home placement of child for over one year.

Colorado

The Law	West's Colorado Revised Statutes Annotated. ***Example:*** Colorado Revised Statutes Annotated, Title 14, Article 10, Section 14-10-106 (C.R.S.A. Sec. 14-10-106).
Case Style	IN THE DISTRICT COURT IN AND FOR THE COUNTY OF _____ AND STATE OF COLORADO
Designation of Parties	_____, Petitioner, vs. _____, Respondent.
Custody	Factors: Best interest of the child, considering: (1) parties' wishes; (2) child's wishes; (3) interaction and interrelationship between the child and the parties, siblings, and other significant persons; (4) child's adjustment to home, school, and community; (5) mental and physical health of all persons involved; (6) custodian's ability to encourage sharing, love, affection, and contact with the other party; (7) evidence of the parties ability to cooperate and make joint decisions; (8) evidence of each party's ability to encourage sharing, love, affection, and contact with the other party; (9) whether the past pattern of involvement of the parties with the child reflects a system of values, time commitment, and mutual support that would indicate an ability as joint custodians to provide a positive and nourishing relationship with the child;

(10) physical proximity of the parties as it relates to practical considerations of awarding joint custody; (11) whether joint custody will promote more frequent or continuing contacts; (12) any history of child abuse or neglect; and, (13) any history of spouse abuse.

Child Support

State child support guidelines and tables are found in C.R.S.A. Sec. 14-10-115. Termination age: 21.

Termination of
Parental Rights

Grounds: (1) emotional or mental illness or mental deficiency of parent; (2) physical or sexual abuse of the child by the parent; (3) violent behavior of parent; (4) substance abuse by the parent; and, (5) neglect of the child by the parent.

Connecticut

The Law	Connecticut General Statutes Annotated. **Example:** Connecticut General Statutes Annotated, Title 46b, Section 46b-40 (C.G.S.A. Sec. 46b-40). Ignore "chapter" numbers.
Case Style	IN THE SUPERIOR COURT OF THE STATE OF CONNECTICUT
Designation of Parties	_____, Plaintiff, vs. _____, Defendant.
Custody	Best interest of the child considering wishes of the child, if sufficient age. Law favors joint custody if both parties agree.
Child Support	Factors: (1) age, health, station, occupation, earning capacity, amount and sources of income, estate, vocational skills and employability of the parties and (2) child's age, health, station, occupation, educational status and expectation, amount and sources of income, vocational skills, employability, estate, and needs. Termination age: 18.
Termination of Parental Rights	Grounds: (1) abandonment and (2) neglect.

Delaware

The Law   Delaware Code Annotated.
Example: Delaware Code Annotated, Title 13, Section 1502 (D.C.A. 13 Sec. 1502).

Case Style   IN THE FAMILY COURT OF THE STATE OF DELAWARE IN AND FOR _____ COUNTY

Designation of Parties   _____, Petitioner, vs.
_____, Respondent.

Custody   Determined by the best interest of the child, considering: (1) wishes of the parents and the child, (2) interaction and interrelationship of the child with parents, siblings, and other significant persons; (3) child's adjustment to home, school, and community; and, (4) mental and physical health of all persons involved.

Child Support   Factors: (1) health, relative economic condition, financial circumstances, and income of the parties and child and (2) general equities inherent in the situation. Formula and forms may be found in Family Court Civil Rules, Rule 52(c) and Forms 509 and 509p.
Termination age: 18.

(continued)

Termination of
Parental Rights

Grounds: (1) abandonment; (2) parents are mentally incompetent; (3) parent convicted of a felony in which child was a victim or involved harm to child; and, (4) parents unable or failed to provide for physical, mental or emotional welfare of child.

District of Columbia

The Law	District of Columbia Code. **Example:** District of Columbia Code, Title 16, Section 901 (D.C.C. Sec. 16-901).
Case Style	IN THE SUPERIOR COURT OF THE DISTRICT OF COLUMBIA — FAMILY DIVISION
Designation of Parties	_____, Plaintiff, vs. _____, Defendant.
Custody	Best interest of the child considering: (1) wishes of the child; (2) wishes of the parties; (3) the interaction and interrelationship between the child and parents, siblings, and other significant persons; (4) child's adjustment to home, school, and community; and, (5) mental and physical health of all persons involved.
Child Support	State child support guidelines found in D.C.C. Sec. 16-916.1. Termination age: 18.
Termination of Parental Rights	Grounds: (1) physical, mental, and emotional health of parent that affect the child's welfare and (2) substance abuse by parent.

Florida

The Law

Florida Statutes.

Example: Florida Statutes, Chapter 61, Section 61.001 (F.S. Sec. 61.001). A new set of statute books is published in odd-numbered years, and supplemental volumes even-numbered years. You may also find West's Florida Statutes Annotated, with pocket part supplements. Most current changes are found in soft-cover volumes of Florida Session Laws, published at the end of each legislative session. Florida has many official forms, found in the Florida Rules of Court, or obtained from the court clerk.

Case Style

IN THE CIRCUIT COURT OF THE _____ JUDICIAL [Each circuit has a number] CIRCUIT, IN AND FOR _____ COUNTY, FLORIDA

Designation of Parties

_____, Petitioner, vs.
_____, Respondent.

Custody

Joint custody (referred to as "joint parental responsibility") is preferred, and must be ordered unless judge finds it would be detrimental to the child. Generally this refers to joint responsibility for making decisions for the child's welfare, with one party's home being designated as the "primary residence." Responsibility and primary residence determined by the best interest of the child considering: (1) which party is more likely to allow frequent and continuing contact with the other party; (2) love, affection, and other emotional ties existing between the child and each party; (3) each party's capacity and disposition to provide food, clothing, medical care, or other material needs for the child; (4) length of time the child has been in a stable, satisfactory environment, and the desirability of maintaining continuity; (5) the permanence, as a family unit, of the existing or proposed custodial home; (6) moral fitness of the parties; (7) mental and physical health of the parties; (8) child's home, school, and community record; (9) preference of the child, if sufficient intelligence, understanding, and experience; and, (10) any other relevant factor.

Child Support

State child support guidelines may be found in F.S. Sec. 61.30.
Termination age: 18.

Termination of Parental Rights

Grounds: (1) abandonment; (2) conduct of parent which threatens life or well-being of the child; (3) parent is incarcerated in state or federal prison; and, (4) parent engages in egregious conduct which threatens health or safety of child.

Georgia

The Law	Official Code of Georgia Annotated. **Example:** Official Code of Georgia Annotated, Title 19, Chapter 5, Section 1 (C.G.A. Sec. 19-5-1).

Case Style

IN THE SUPERIOR COURT OF
_____,
GEORGIA

Designation
of Parties

_____, Petitioner, vs.
_____, Respondent.

Custody

No specific factors or provisions for joint custody in statute. Child may select parent to live with if at least 14 years of age.

Child Support

Basically figured as a percent of the payor's gross income, as follows: 17% to 23% for one child; 23% to 28% for two children; 25% to 32% for three children; 29% to 35% for four children; and, 31% to 37% for five or more children. This can be modified by special circumstances. Guidelines found at C.G.A. Sec. 19-6-15. Termination age: 18.

Termination of
Parental Rights

Grounds: (1) abandonment; (2) mental, physical, and emotional health that renders parent unable to care for child; (3) excessive use of alcohol or drugs; (4) conviction of a felony that adversely affects parent/child relationship; (5) physical, mental, or emotional neglect of child; (6) egregious conduct of parent toward the child; and, (7) death of a sibling that constitutes evidence that death resulted from neglect or abuse by parent.

Hawaii

The Law	Hawaii Revised Statutes. ***Example:*** Hawaii Revised Statutes, Title 580, Section 580-41 (H.R.S. Sec. 580-41).
Case Style	IN THE FAMILY COURT OF THE _____ JUDICIAL CIRCUIT
Designation *of Parties*	_____, Plaintiff, vs. _____, Defendant.
Custody	Best interest of the child considering: (1) child's wishes, if of sufficient age and capacity to reason and (2) any evidence of family violence.
Child Support	State child support guidelines found at H.R.S. Sec. 576D-7. Termination age: 18.
Termination of *Parental Rights*	Grounds: Abandonment.

Idaho

The Law	Idaho Code. ***Example:*** Idaho Code, Title 32, Chapter 6, Section 32-601 (I.C. Sec. 32-601).
Case Style	IN THE DISTRICT COURT OF THE _____ [Each circuit has a number] JUDICIAL DISTRICT FOR THE STATE OF IDAHO, IN AND FOR THE COUNTY OF _____
Designation of Parties	_____, Plaintiff, vs. _____, Defendant.
Custody	Best interest of the child considering: (1) wishes of parties; (2) wishes of child; (3) interaction and interrelationship between the child and parties, siblings, or other significant persons; (4) adjustment to home, school, and community; (5) mental and physical health of all persons involved; (6) need to promote continuity and stability in the child's life; and, (7) any history of domestic violence. Joint custody is presumed best, unless either party can show otherwise.
Child Support	State child support guidelines issued by Idaho Supreme Court (obtain from court clerk or law library). Termination age: 18.
Termination of Parental Rights	Grounds: (1) abandonment; (2) neglect or abuse of child by parent; and, (3) mental illness or mental deficiency of parent.

Illinois

The Law	West's Smith-Hurd Illinois Compiled Statutes Annotated. *Example:* Illinois Compiled Statutes, Chapter 750, Act 5, Section 5/101 (750 ILCS 5/101).
Case Style	IN THE CIRCUIT COURT OF THE _____ [each district has a number] JUDICIAL DISTRICT, _____ COUNTY, ILLINOIS
Designation of Parties	_____, Petitioner, vs. _____, Respondent.
Custody	Factors: (1) wishes of parents and child; (2) interaction and interrelationship between the child and the parents, siblings, and other significant persons; (3) child's adjustment to home, school, and community; (4) mental and physical health of parties and child; (5) any physical threat to child; and, (6) each party's willingness to encourage and facilitate continued contact between the other parent and the child.
Child Support	Basically a percentage of the payor's net income, as follows: 20% for one child; 25% for two children; 32% for three children; 40% for four children; 45% for five children; and, 50% for six or more children. Other factors for special needs are listed, which may justify more or less. Guidelines found at 750 ILCS 5/505. Termination age: 18.
Termination of Parental Rights	Grounds: Abuse.

Indiana

The Law	West's Annotated Indiana Code. ***Example:*** Annotated Indiana Code, Title 31, Article3 1, Chapter 11.5, Section 1 (A.I.C. Sec. 31-1-11.5-1).
Case Style	_____ COURT OF _____ COUNTY, INDIANA [The first blank will either be "SUPERIOR," "CIRCUIT," or "DOMESTIC RELATIONS," depending upon the particular county you file in.]
Designation of Parties	_____, Petitioner, vs. _____, Respondent.
Custody	Factors: (1) age and sex of the child; (2) wishes of the parents and child; (3) interaction and interrelationship between the child and the parents, siblings, and other significant persons; (4) child's adjustment to home, school, and community; and, (5) mental and physical health of all persons involved. Joint legal custody may be awarded.
Child Support	Factors: (1) financial resources of custodial parent; (2) physical and mental condition of the child and the child's educational needs; (3) financial resources and needs of the noncustodial parent; and, (4) any special educational or medical needs of the child. Termination age: 18.

(continued)

Termination of
Parental Rights

Grounds: (1) abandonment; (2) parent judicially declared incompetent or mentally defective; and, (3) best interest of the child.

Iowa

The Law	Iowa Code Annotated. ***Example:*** Iowa Code Annotated, Section 598.1 (I.C.A. Sec. 598.1).
Case Style	IN THE DISTRICT COURT OF THE STATE OF IOWA IN AND FOR _____ COUNTY
Designation *of Parties*	_____, Petitioner, vs. _____, Respondent.
Custody	Best interest of the child "which will assure the child opportunity for the maximum continuing physical and emotional contact with both parents." Either party may request joint legal custody. If the judge refuses, findings must be in decree, considering various factors in the statute.
Child Support	State child support guidelines found at I.C.A. Sec. 598.21. Termination age: 18.
Termination of *Parental Rights*	Grounds: (1) abandonment; (2) abuse or neglect of child; (3) parent imprisoned for crime against the child; (4) parent has a chronic mental illness and presents a danger to self and others; and, (5) substance abuse.

Kansas

The Law Kansas Statutes Annotated.

Example: Kansas Statutes Annotated, Section 60-1601 (K.S.A. Sec. 60-1601). You may find these volumes as either "Vernon's Kansas Statutes Annotated," or "Kansas Statutes Annotated, Official." Both sets have very poor indexes.

Case Style IN THE DISTRICT COURT IN AND FOR THE COUNTY OF

_____, KANSAS

Designation _____, Petitioner, vs.
of Parties _____, Respondent.

Custody Best interest of the child considering: (1) any agreement of the parties; (2) length of time child has been under actual care and control of any person other than a parent and the circumstances involved; (3) desires of the parties; (4) desires of the child; (5) interaction and interrelationship between child and parties, siblings, and other significant persons; (6) child's adjustment to home, school, and community; (7) each party's willingness and ability to respect and appreciate the bond between the child and the other party; (8) any evidence of spousal abuse; and, (9) any other relevant factor.

Child Support

Supreme Court Child Support Guidelines may be obtained from court clerk or law library. Termination age: 18.

Termination of Parental Rights

Grounds: (1) emotional or mental illness, mental deficiency, or physical disability of parent; (2) physical, emotional, or sexual abuse of child; (3) substance abuse; (4) physical, mental, or emotional neglect of child; (5) conviction of a felony and imprisonment; and, (6) unexplained injury or death of another child of the parent.

Kentucky

The Law

Kentucky Revised Statutes.
Example: Kentucky Revised Statutes, Chapter 403, Section 010 (K.R.S. Sec. 403.010).

Case Style

_____ CIRCUIT COURT, KENTUCKY [County name goes in blank]

Designation
of Parties

_____, Petitioner, vs.
_____, Respondent.

Custody

Best interest of the child, considering: (1) wishes of the parents and child; (2) interaction and interrelationship between the child and parents, siblings, and other significant persons; (3) child's adjustment to home, school, and community; and, (4) mental and physical condition of all persons involved. Judge may grant joint custody in the child's best interest.

Child Support

State child support guidelines found at K.R.S. Sec. 403.212. Termination age: 18.

Termination of
Parental Rights

Grounds: (1) abandonment; (2) physical or emotional abuse of the child; (3) sexual abuse of the child; (4) failure or inability to provide parental care and protection; and, (5) failure to provide food, clothes, and shelter for the child for reasons other than poverty.

Louisiana

The Law

West's Louisiana Statutes Annotated. Some will be titled with the abbreviation "LSA." The books containing the laws of Louisiana are one of the more complicated sets of any state. They are divided into subjects, so you need to be sure you have the properly labeled set, such as "Civil Code," "Revised Statutes," or "Code of Civil Procedure."
Example: LSA Civil Code, Article 102 (C.C., Art. 102). Ask the law librarian if you need assistance.

Case Style

_____ JUDICIAL DISTRICT COURT, PARISH OF _____, LOUISIANA [District number goes in first blank]

Designation of Parties

_____, Plaintiff, vs.
_____, Defendant.

Custody

Joint legal custody is preferred and presumed best for the child. Parties must submit a joint custody plan. If one party requests sole custody, he or she must prove it is in the child's best interest considering the following factors: (1) the child's love, affection, and emotional ties with each parent; (2) capacity and disposition of the parties to give love, affection, guidance, education, and religious guidance; (3) capacity and disposition of the parties to give the child food, clothing, medical care, etc.; (4) length of time

(continued)

the child has been in a stable, satisfactory environment, and the desirability for continuity; (5) permanence as a family unit for existing or proposed home; (6) moral fitness of the parties; (7) mental and physical health of the parties; (8) home, school, and community record of the child; (9) preference of the child, if the child is of sufficient age; (10) willingness of each party to facilitate a relationship between the child and the opposing party; (11) distances between the parties residences; and, (12) any other factor the judge decides is proper.

Child Support

Based upon (1) needs of the child; and (2) actual resources of each parent. Guidelines found in LSA Revised Statutes, 9:315. Termination age: 18.

Termination of Parental Rights

Grounds: (1) misconduct of parent toward the child that constitutes extreme abuse, cruel and inhuman treatment, or grossly neglectful behavior; (2) abuse or neglect that is life threatening; and, (3) abandonment.

Maine

The Law	Page's Maine Revised Statutes Annotated. **Example:** Maine Revised Statutes Annotated, Title 19, Section 661 (19 M.R.S.A. Sec. 661).

Case Style

STATE OF MAINE, _____
COURT _____ COUNTY
[First blank is for either "DISTRICT" or "SUPERIOR"]

*Designation
of Parties*

_____, Plaintiff, vs.
_____, Defendant.

Custody

Best interest of child considering: (1) child's age; (2) child's relationship with each party and other significant persons; (3) preference of child, if suitable age and maturity; (4) duration and adequacy of child's current living arrangement and desirability of maintaining continuity; (5) stability of proposed living arrangement; (6) motivation of the parties and their capacity to give love, affection and guidance; (7) child's adjustment to home, school, and community; (8) each party's capacity to allow and encourage a relationship between the child and the other party; (9) each party's capacity to cooperate in child care; (10) the methods of assisting parental cooperation and resolving disputes and each party's willingness to use those methods; (11) effect on the child if one party has sole authority regarding upbringing; (12) any history of domestic abuse; and, (13) any other relevant factor.

(continued)

Child Support	State child support guidelines available from court clerk. Termination age: 18.
Termination of Parental Rights	Grounds: (1) abandonment; (2) parent has acted toward a child in a way that is heinous or abhorrent to society; and, (3) parent was convicted of a felony in which the child was a victim.

Maryland

The Law	Annotated Code of Maryland.

The Law — Annotated Code of Maryland.
Example: Annotated Code of Maryland, Family Law, Section 7-101 (A.C.M., Family Law Sec. 7-101). Volumes are arranged by subject, so be sure you have the correctly titled volume.

Case Style — IN THE CIRCUIT COURT FOR _____ COUNTY, MARYLAND

Designation of Parties — _____, Plaintiff, vs. _____, Defendant.

Custody — There are no statutory factors.

Child Support — State child support guidelines and table found in A.C.M., Family Law Secs. 12-201 and 12-204. Termination age: 18.

Termination of Parental Rights — Grounds: (1) child has been out of the custody of the natural parents for over one year; (2) parent has been convicted of child abuse; and, (3) parent has been convicted of a crime of violence and imprisoned for at least ten years.

Massachusetts

The Law	Annotated Laws of Massachusetts. ***Example:*** Annotated Laws of Massachusetts, Chapter 208, Section 1 (A.L.M., C208, Sec. 1).
Case Style	COMMONWEALTH OF MASSACHUSETTS, _____ COURT
Designation of Parties	_____, Plaintiff, vs. _____, Defendant.
Custody	No factors in statute; only general concepts including best interests of the child.
Child Support	State child support guidelines available from court clerk. Termination age: 18.
Termination of Parental Rights	Grounds: (1) abandonment; (2) child or sibling abused or neglected by parent; (3) parent fails to provide child proper care or custody; (4) severe or repetitive conduct toward the child of a physically, emotionally or sexually abusive or neglectful nature; and, (5) felony conviction of parent.

Michigan

The Law

Michigan Statutes Annotated (M.S.A.) or Michigan Compiled Laws Annotated (M.C.L.A). Michigan has two official sets of laws, each from a different publisher. **Example:** M.S.A. Sec. 25.96(1) or M.C.L.A. Sec. 552.16a.

Case Style

STATE OF MICHIGAN _____ JUDICIAL CIRCUIT, _____ COUNTY [Circuit number in first blank]

Designation of Parties

_____, Complainant, vs.
_____, Defendant.

Custody

Best interest of child, considering the following factors: (1) love, affection, and other emotional ties existing between the parties and the child; (2) the capacity and disposition of each to give love, affection, guidance, and continuation of education and raising the child in his or her religion; (3) the capacity and disposition of each to provide food, clothing, and medical care; (4) length of time the child has lived in a stable, satisfactory environment and the desirability of maintaining continuity; (5) permanence as a family unit of the existing or proposed custodial home; (6) moral fitness of the parties; (7) mental and physical health of the parties and the child; (8) home, school, and community record of the child; (9) preference of the child, if of suitable age; (10) willingness and ability
(continued)

of the parties to facilitate and encourage a relationship between the child and the other parent; and, (11) any other relevant factor. Joint custody may be considered.

Child Support

Child support may continue beyond age of 18 if the child is regularly attending high school on a full-time basis, with a reasonable expectation of graduating while residing with the custodial parent; but in no event beyond the age of 19 years, 6 months. Termination age: 18.

Termination of Parental Rights

Grounds: (1) abandonment; (2) physical injury, physical or sexual abuse by parent; (3) parent fails to provide proper care or custody for the child; (4) parent imprisoned for such a period that child will be deprived of normal home life; (5) parental rights terminated due to serious and chronic neglect or abuse; and, (6) child will be harmed if returned to parent.

Minnesota

The Law	Minnesota Statutes Annotated.

Example: Minnesota Statutes Annotated, Section 518.002 (M.S.A. Sec. 518.002).

Case Style

STATE OF MINNESOTA DISTRICT COURT COUNTY OF _____, _____ JUDICIAL DISTRICT [each district has a number]

Designation of Parties

_____, Petitioner, vs.

_____, Respondent.

Custody

Factors: (1) the parties' wishes; (2) child's preference, if of sufficient age; (3) child's primary caretaker; (4) intimacy of the relationship between child and each party; (5) interaction and interrelationship between child and the parties, siblings, and other significant persons; (6) child's adjustment to home, school, and community; (7) length of time in a stable, satisfactory environment and desirability of maintaining continuity; (8) permanence, as a family unit, of the existing or proposed home; (9) mental and physical health of all persons involved; (10) each party's capacity and disposition to give love, affection, and guidance and to continue educating and raising the child in the child's culture and religion, if any; (11) child's cultural background; (12) effect of any domestic violence on the child; and, (13) any other relevant factor. Additional considerations when joint custody is

(continued)

requested. See M.S.A. Sec. 518.179 for list of criminal acts that will prohibit an award of custody.

Child Support

State child support guidelines found in M.S.A. Sec. 518.551.
Termination age: 18.

Termination of Parental Rights

Grounds: (1) abandonment; (2) parent refused or neglected to comply with duties imposed upon a parent; (3) parent is palpably unfit to be a party to the parent/child relationship; (4) child adjudicated in need of protection; (5) parental rights as one or more children involuntarily terminated; (6) parent diagnosed as chemically dependent; (7) child experienced severe harm in parent's care; and, (8) child placed in foster care due to parental neglect.

Mississippi

The Law	Mississippi Code 1972 Annotated. **Example:** Mississippi Code, Section 93-5-1 (M.C. Sec. 93-5-1).
Case Style	CHANCERY COURT OF _____ COUNTY, STATE OF MISSISSIPPI
Designation of Parties	_____, COMPLAINANT, vs. _____, DEFENDANT.
Custody	No statutory factors. Child may choose if at least age 12. Presumption in favor of joint custody, both physical and decision making. Judge may require custody plan from parties.
Child Support	No statutory factors. Generally, child support is determined by the relative and proportionate incomes and abilities of the parties. Termination age: 21.
Termination of Parental Rights	Grounds: (1) abandonment; (2) parent responsible for series of abusive incidents concerning the child; (3) substance abuse by the parent; (4) parent suffers from severe mental deficiencies or mental illness; and, (5) parent convicted of physical or sexual abuse against child.

Missouri

The Law	Vernon's Annotated Missouri Statutes. **Example:** Annotated Missouri Statutes, Chapter 452, Section 452.300 (A.M.S. Sec. 452.300).
Case Style	IN THE CIRCUIT COURT _____ COUNTY, MISSOURI
Designation of Parties	_____, Petitioner, vs. _____, Respondent.
Custody	Best interest of the child considering: (1) wishes of the parties; (2) wishes of the child; (3) interaction and interrelationship between child and parties, siblings, and other significant persons; (4) child's adjustment to home, school, and community; (5) mental and physical health, and any abuse history, of all persons involved; (6) child's needs for continuing relationship with both parties, and the ability and willingness of each to actively perform their duties as mother and father for the needs of the child; (7) any intention of either party to relocate outside the state; (8) which party is more likely to allow frequent and meaningful contact between the child and the other party; and, (9) any other relevant factor.

Child Support	Factors: (1) financial needs and resources of the child; (2) financial resources and needs of the parties; (3) standard of living child would have had if no divorce; and, (4) child's physical and emotional condition and educational needs. Termination age: 18.
Termination of Parental Rights	Grounds: (1) abandonment; (2) child has been abused or neglected; (3) parent has been found guilty of a felony violation in which child or sibling was victim; (4) child was conceived as a result of rape; and, (5) parent unfit because of substance abuse.

Montana

The Law

Montana Code Annotated.
Example: Montana Code Annotated, Title 40, Chapter 4, Section 40-4-101 (M.C.A. Sec. 40-4-101).

Case Style

DISTRICT COURT FOR THE STATE OF MONTANA AND FOR THE COUNTY OF_____

Designation of Parties

_____, Petitioner, vs.
_____, Respondent.

Custody

Factors: (1) parties' wishes; (2) child's wishes; (3) interaction and interrelationship between child and parties, siblings, and other significant persons; (4) child's adjustment to home, school, and community (5) mental and physical condition of all persons involved; (6) any physical abuse, or threat of physical abuse, against a party or the child; (7) any chemical dependency or abuse of either party; and, (8) any other relevant factor. Joint custody may be granted but parties will be required to submit to custody plan.

Child Support

Factors: (1) child' financial resources; (2) custodial parent's financial resources; (3) child's physical and emotional condition and educational and medical needs; (4) noncustodial parent's financial resources and needs; (5) child's age; (6) cost of day care; (7) custody arrangements; and, (8) needs of any other person either party is obligated to support.
Termination age: 18.

Termination of Parental Rights

Grounds: (1) parent is unfit; (2) relationship of parent and child doesn't exist; and, (3) parent has irrevocably waived parental rights.

Nebraska

The Law	Revised Statutes of Nebraska. **Example:** Revised Statutes of Nebraska, Chapter 42, Article 3, Section 42-301 (R.S.N. Sec. 42-301).
Case Style	IN THE DISTRICT COURT FOR _____ COUNTY, NEBRASKA
Designation of Parties	_____, Petitioner, vs. _____, Respondent.
Custody	Best interest of the child considering: (1) the relationship of the child and each party; (2) reasonable desires of the child; and, (3) the general health, welfare, and social behavior of the child. Shared or joint custody is possible if both parties agree and a hearing shows it is in the best interest of the child.
Child Support	The state's child support guidelines available from court clerk. Termination age: 19.
Termination of Parental Rights	Grounds: (1) abandonment; (2) child substantially and continuously neglected by parent; (3) parent neglected to provide child with necessary subsistence; (4) parents are unfit by reason of debauchery, habitual use of alcohol or drugs; and, (5) parent is unable to perform responsibilities because of mental illness or deficiency.

Nevada

The Law

Nevada Revised Statutes Annotated.
Example: Nevada Revised Statutes Annotated, Chapter 125, Section 125.010 (N.R.S.A. Sec. 125.010).

Case Style

IN THE DISTRICT COURT FOR _____ COUNTY, NEVADA

Designation of Parties

_____, Plaintiff, vs.
_____, Defendant.

Custody

Best interest of the child considering: (1) which party is more likely to allow frequent association and continuing relationship with the other party; (2) wishes of the child, if of sufficient age and intelligence; (3) "any nomination by a parent of a guardian for the child"; and, (4) whether either party has engaged in an act of domestic violence against the child, the other party, or other person residing with the child. Preference is for joint custody.

Child Support

Based upon the following percentage of gross income: 18% for one child; 25% for two children; 29% for three children; 31% for four children; and, an additional 2% for each additional child. Minimum support of $100 per month per child, unless the judge finds the payor is unable to pay that amount. Any deviation from these percentages, even when the parties agree, must be explained in the decree, by considering: (1) extraordinary needs of the child are not being met; (2) cost of health insurance; (3) cost of child care; (4) special educational needs; (5) age of child; (6) the parties' other support obligations; (7) value of services contributed by either party; (8) any public assistance paid to support the child; (9) expenses reasonably related to pregnancy and confinement; (10) cost of transportation for visitation if custodial parent moved from the jurisdiction of the court; (11) amount of time child spends with each party; (12) other necessary expenses for the child's benefit; and, (13) the parties relative income. Termination age: 18.

Termination of Parental Rights

Grounds: (1) abandonment; (2) neglect of the child; (3) unfitness of the parent; (4) failure of parental adjustment; and, (5) risk of physical, mental, or emotional injury to child if the child remains with the parent.

New Hampshire

The Law	New Hampshire Revised Statutes Annotated. *Example:* New Hampshire Revised Statutes Annotated, Chapter 458, Section 458:4 (N.H.R.S.A. Sec. 458:4).
Case Style	THE STATE OF NEW HAMPSHIRE, SUPERIOR COURT IN AND FOR _____ COUNTY
Designation of Parties	_____, Petitioner, vs. _____, Respondent.
Custody	Joint legal custody is presumed in the child's best interest, unless abuse is shown. Final order must state reasons if joint legal custody is not ordered. Factors: (1) preference of the child and (2) any domestic violence.
Child Support	Needs based on a percentage of the parties' combined net income as follows: 25% for one child; 33% for two children; 40% for three children; and, 45% for four or more children. Each party responsible for a pro rata share of the needs according to income. Termination age: 18.

Termination of
Parental Rights

Grounds: (1) abandonment; (2) parent has neglected to provide the child with necessary subsistence; (3) child neglect or abuse; (4) mental deficiency or mental illness rendering parent incapable of giving child proper parental care; (5) parent knowingly or willingly caused sexual, physical, emotional, or mental abuse of child; and, (6) incarceration of parent for a felony.

New Jersey

The Law

NJSA (New Jersey Statutes Annotated). *Example:* NJSA, Title 2A, Chapter 34, Section 2A:34-2 (NJSA Sec. 2A:34-2).

Case Style

SUPERIOR COURT OF NEW JERSEY, CHANCERY DIVISION, FAMILY PART, _____ COUNTY

Designation of Parties

_____, Plaintiff, vs.

_____, Defendant.

Custody

Best interest of the child considering the following factors: (1) parent's ability to agree, communicate, and cooperate in matters relating to the child; (2) parents' willingness to accept custody and facilitate visitation; (3) interaction and interrelationship between the child and parents and siblings; (4) any history of domestic violence; (5) preference of child; if of suitable age; (6) needs of child; (7) stability of home environment offered; (8) quality and continuity of education; (9) fitness of parents; (10) geographical proximity of the parties' homes; (11) extent and quality of time with the child before and after separation; (12) employment responsibilities; and, (13) age and number of children. Judge must follow the parties agreement, unless he or she determines it is not in the child's best interest. When parties don't agree, the judge may require each party to submit a proposed custody plan.

Child Support

(1) needs of child; (2) standard of living and economic circumstances; (3) income and assets of parties; (4) earning ability of the parties; (5) child's need and capacity for education, including higher education; (6) age and health of parties and child; (7) income, assets, and earning capacity of child; (8) other child support obligations of parties; (9) debts and liabilities of parties and child; and, (10) any other relevant factor.

Termination age: 18.

*Termination of
Parental Rights*

Grounds: (1) child's health and development has been endangered by the parental relationship; (2) parent cannot or will not provide a safe and stable home for the child; (3) termination of parental rights will not do more harm than good; and, (4) abandonment.

New Mexico

The Law

New Mexico Statutes 1978 Annotated.
Example: New Mexico Statutes Annotated, Chapter 40, Section 40-4-1 (N.M.S.A. Sec. 40-4-1).

Case Style

_____ JUDICIAL DISTRICT [each district has a number] COURT COUNTY OF _____, STATE OF NEW MEXICO

Designation
of Parties

_____, Petitioner, vs.
_____, Respondent.

Custody

Best interest of the child considering: (1) wishes of parties; (2) wishes of child; (3) interaction and interrelationship between the child and parties, siblings, and other significant persons; (4) child's adjustment to home, school, and community; and, (5) mental and physical condition of all persons involved. Joint custody is presumed in the child's best interest considering: (1) whether child has established a close relationship with each party; (2) whether each party is capable of providing care; (3) whether each party is willing to accept responsibilities of child care; (4) whether child can best maintain and strengthen a relationship with both parties and profit from such involvement; (5) whether each party is able to allow the other to provide care without intrusion; (6) the suitability of the parenting plan; (7) geographical distance between the parties' residences; and, (8) the parties' willingness and ability to communicate and cooperate regarding the child's needs.

Child Support   State child support guidelines available from court clerk.
Termination age: 18.

Termination of   Grounds: (1) abandonment; (2) neglect
Parental Rights   or abuse of the child; and, (3) child placed in the permanent care of others.

New York

The Law	McKinney's Consolidated Laws of New York Annotated. *Example:* Consolidated Laws of New York, Domestic Relations Law, Section 170 (C.L.N.Y., D.R.L. Sec. 170). These volumes are first divided into subjects, so be sure you find the correctly titled volumes, such as "Domestic Relations," "Estates, Powers and Trusts," "Probate," etc.
Case Style	SUPREME COURT OF THE STATE OF NEW YORK _____ COUNTY
Designation of Parties	_____, Plaintiff, vs. _____, Defendant.
Custody	Best interest of the child.
Child Support	Based on a pro rata share of the child's needs, according to the relative income of the parties. Needs are determined as a percentage of the parties' combined income as follows: 17% for one child; 25% for two children; 29% for three children; 31% for four children; and, 35% or more for five or more children. This amount may be increased if certain special circumstances exist as stated in the state statute. Termination age: 21.
Termination of Parental Rights	Grounds: (1) abandonment; (2) parent surrender the child to an authorized agency; and, (3) mental illness or mental retardation that renders parent incapable of taking care of the child.

North Carolina

The Law

General Statutes of North Carolina.
Example: General Statutes of North Carolina, Chapter 50, Section 1 (G.S.N.C. Sec. 50-1). (Lawyers and judges commonly refer to these as the "North Carolina General Statutes," although that is not the title that appears on the covers of the volumes.)

Case Style

STATE OF NORTH CAROLINA, FAMILY COURT _____ DIVISION
[Check with court clerk for division designation]

Designation
of Parties

_____, Plaintiff, vs.
_____, Defendant.

Custody

Best interest of the child.

Child Support

State child support guidelines available from court clerk.
Termination age: 18.

Termination of
Parental Rights

Grounds: (1) parent has neglected or abused the child; (2) parent has willfully left child in foster care for more than twelve months; (3) parent is incapable of providing proper care and supervision for the child; and, (4) abandonment.

North Dakota

The Law	North Dakota Century Code Annotated. ***Example***: North Dakota Century Code, Title 14, Chapter 14-05, Section 14-05-01 (N.D.C.C. Sec. 14-05-01).

Case Style

STATE OF NORTH DAKOTA, COUNTY OF _____ IN THE DISTRICT COURT, _____ JUDICIAL DISTRICT [each district has a number]

Designation of Parties

_____, Plaintiff, vs.
_____, Defendant.

Custody

(1) love, affection, and emotional ties between child and each party; (2) each party's capacity and disposition to give love, affection, and guidance and to continue the child's education; (3) each party's disposition to provide food, clothing, medical care, and other material needs; (4) length of time the child has been in a stable, satisfactory environment and the desirability of maintaining continuity; (5) the permanence, as a family unit, of the existing or proposed custodial home; (6) moral fitness of the parties; (7) mental and physical health of the parties; (8) child's home, school, and community record; (9) the reasonable preference of the child, if of sufficient intelligence, understanding, and experience; (10) an existence of domestic violence; (11) the interaction and interrelationship between

the child and parties, siblings, and other significant persons; and, (12) any other relevant factor.

Child Support

State child support guidelines available from court clerk.
Termination age: 18.

Termination of
Parental Rights

Grounds: (1) neglect by reason of misconduct, faults, or habits of parent; (2) by reason of physical or mental incapacity the parent is unable to care for the child; and, (3) child suffers from mental, moral, or emotional harm.

Ohio

The Law	Page's Ohio Revised Code Annotated. **Example:** Ohio Revised Code, Title 31, Section 3105.01 (O.R.C. Sec. 3105.01).
Case Style	IN THE COURT OF COMMON PLEAS OF _____ COUNTY, OHIO
Designation of Parties	_____, Plaintiff, vs. _____, Defendant.
Custody	Best interest of the child, considering: (1) wishes of the parties; (2) child's wishes, if interviewed by judge; (3) the interaction and interrelationship between the child and parties, siblings, and other significant persons; (4) child's adjustment to home, school, and community; (5) mental and physical condition of all persons involved; (6) party more likely to honor and facilitate visitation; (7) compliance with any child support orders; (8) any history of abuse or neglect; (9) any history of visitation denial; and, (10) whether a party intends to make his or her residence outside of Ohio.

Child Support

(1) child's resources and earning ability; (2) parties' resources and assets; (3) physical and emotional condition and needs of child; (4) child's need and capacity for education; (5) child's age; (6) parties' other support obligations; and, (7) value of services contributed by custodial parent. Child support order must provide for medical insurance payment through the child support enforcement agency and one of the income withholding orders or cash bonds.

Termination age: 18.

Termination of
Parental Rights

Grounds: (1) abandonment and (2) abuse and neglect.

Oklahoma

The Law	Oklahoma Statutes Annotated. ***Example:*** Oklahoma Statutes Annotated, Title 43, Section 101 (43 O.S.A. Sec. 101).
Case Style	STATE OF OKLAHOMA, IN THE DISTRICT COURT, _____ COUNTY
Designation of Parties	_____, Plaintiff, vs. _____, Defendant.
Custody	(1) physical, mental, and moral welfare of the child and (2) child's preference. If domestic violence is involved it is presumed that it is against the best interest of the child for the guilty party to have custody.
Child Support	Factors: (1) income and means of the parties and (2) the property and assets of the parties. Termination age: 18.
Termination of Parental Rights	Grounds: (1) abandonment; (2) child has been adjudicated to be deprived; (3) best interest of the child; (4) parent convicted of criminal act relating to child abuse or neglect; (5) physical or sexual abuse of child by parent; and, (6) parent has a mental illness or deficiency that renders him or her incapable of caring for the child.

Oregon

The Law	Oregon Revised Statutes Annotated. **Example:** Oregon Revised Statutes, Chapter 107, Section 107.015 (O.R.S. Sec. 107.015).

Case Style

IN THE CIRCUIT COURT
THE STATE OF OREGON
THE COUNTY OF

_____

Designation
of Parties

_____, Petitioner, vs.
_____, Respondent.

Custody

Joint custody only awarded when both parties agree. Factors: (1) emotional ties between the child and other family members; (2) each party's interest in and attitude toward the child; (3) desirability of continuing existing relationships; and, (4) any abuse of one party by the other. Conduct and lifestyle are only considered if it is causing or may cause emotional orphysical damage to the child (this is usually very difficult to prove).

Child Support

Factors: (1) evidence of the other available resources of a parent; (2) the reasonable necessities of a parent; (3) the net income; (4) parent's ability to borrow; (5) number and needs of other dependents of a parent; (6) medical circumstances of a parent; (7) needs of the child; (8) desirability of the custodial parent

(continued)

remaining in the home as a full-time parent and homemaker; and, (9) tax consequences. Termination age: 18.

Termination of
Parental Rights

Grounds: (1) physical and sexual abuse of the child by the parent; (2) abuse or neglect of any child resulting in death; (3) emotional illness, mental illness, or mental deficiency that renders parent incapable of caring for child; (4) addictive or habitual use of alcohol or drugs; and, (5) neglect of child.

Pennsylvania

The Law	Purdon's Pennsylvania Consolidated Statutes Annotated.
	Example: Pennsylvania Consolidated Statutes Annotated, Title 23, Section 3101 (23 Pa.C.S.A. Sec. 3101).

Case Style

COURT OF COMMON PLEAS, _____ COUNTY, PENNSYLVANIA

Designation of Parties

_____, Plaintiff, vs.
_____, Defendant.

Custody

Best interest of the child based upon which parent is more likely to encourage and allow frequent and continuing contact with the other parent. If joint custody is desired, court may require written custody plan.

Child Support

State child support award based on reasonable needs of the child and ability of parent to provide support. Primary emphasis is placed on net incomes and earning capacities of the parents. Termination age: 21.

Termination of Parental Rights

Grounds: (1) abuse and/or neglect; (2) child removed from parents by the court; and, (3) child conceived as a result of rape or incest; and abandonment.

Rhode Island

The Law	General Laws of Rhode Island. **Example:** General Laws of Rhode Island, Section 15-5-1 (G.L.R.I. Sec. 15-5-1). Ignore "Title" and "Chapter" numbers.
Case Style	STATE OF RHODE ISLAND, FAMILY COURT _____ DIVISION [Check with court clerk for division designation]
Designation of Parties	_____, Plaintiff, vs. _____, Defendant.
Custody	Best interest of the child.
Child Support	Factors: (1) financial resources of the child; (2) financial resources of the custodial parent (3) physical and emotional condition of the child and his or her educational needs; and, (4) financial resources and needs of the noncustodial parent. Termination age: 18.
Termination of Parental Rights	Grounds: (1) parent willfully neglected to provide care and maintenance for child; (2) parent is unfit by reason of conduct or conditions detrimental to the child; (3) emotional illness, mental illness, mental deficiency of the parent; (4) conduct toward any child of a cruel or abusive nature; (5) child has been placed in custody or care of department for children; and, (6) abandonment.

South Carolina

The Law

Code of Laws of South Carolina.
Example: Code of Laws of South Carolina, Title 20, Section 20-3-10 (C.L.S.C. Sec. 20-3-10).

Case Style

STATE OF SOUTH CAROLINA, THE _____ COURT OF THE _____ JUDICIAL DISTRICT [each district has a number]

Designation of Parties

_____, Plaintiff, vs.
_____, Defendant.

Custody

Determined "as from the circumstances of the parties and the nature of the case and the best spiritual as well as other interests of the children as may be fit, equitable and just."

Child Support

Same factors as for custody, and "a fair and reasonable sum according to his or her means, as may be determined by the court." Termination age: 18.

Termination of Parental Rights

Grounds: (1) best interest of the child; (2) child or another child in home harmed as a result of abuse or neglect; (3) abandonment; (4) alcohol and drug addiction; and, (5) parent is mentally deficient or ill and cannot take care of child.

South Dakota

The Law	South Dakota Codified Laws. ***Example:*** South Dakota Codified Laws, Title 25, Chapter 25-4, Section 25-4-1 (S.D.C.L. Sec. 25-4-1).
Case Style	STATE OF SOUTH DAKOTA, COUNTY OF _____, IN THE CIRCUIT COURT, _____ JUDICIAL DISTRICT [each district has a number]
Designation of Parties	_____, Plaintiff, vs. _____, Defendant.
Custody	Only factor referenced in state statute is that custody is to be determined "as may seem necessary and proper."
Child Support	State child support guidelines available at S.D.C.L. Sec. 25-7-6.2. Termination age: 18.
Termination of Parental Rights	Abandonment is the only statutory factor.

Tennessee

The Law

Tennessee Code Annotated.
Example: Tennessee Code Annotated, Title 36, Section 36-4-101 (T.C.A. Sec. 36-4-101).

Case Style

IN THE _____ COURT OF _____ COUNTY, TENNESSEE [check with the circuit clerk for proper court designation]

Designation of Parties

_____, Petitioner, vs.
_____, Respondent.

Custody

Best interests of the child considering the following factors: (1) love, affection and emotional ties between parents and child; (2) disposition of parents to provide food, clothing, medical care, education, and other necessary care and degree to which parent has become the primary caregiver; (3) importance of continuity in the child's life and length of time child has lived in a stable, satisfactory environment; (4) stability of the family unit; (5) mental and physical health of parents; (6) child's home, school, and community record; (7) reasonable preference of child at least 12 years of age; (8) any evidence of physical or emotional abuse of child, parent, or others; and, (9) character and behavior of any person who resides in or frequents the home and that person's interaction with the child.

(continued)

Child Support	State child support guidelines available from court clerk. Termination age: 18.
Termination of Parental Rights	Grounds: (1) best interest of the child; (2) abandonment; (3) child removed from home of parent by order of court; (4) parent committed severe child abuse; (5) parent incarcerated for conduct against the child; (6) parent sentenced to a term of ten or more years in prison; and, (7) parent incompetent to care for child.

Texas

The Law	Vernon's Texas Code Annotated. **Example:** Texas Code Annotated, Family Code, Chapter 3, Section 3.01 (T.C.A., F.C. Sec. 3.01).
Case Style	IN THE DISTRICT COURT OF _____ COUNTY, TEXAS, JUDICIAL DISTRICT _____ [check with the circuit clerk for proper judicial district designation]
Designation of Parties	_____, Petitioner, vs. _____, Respondent.
Custody	Called "managing conservatorship." Factors include: (1) qualifications of the parent and (2) any evidence of intentional use of abusive force against spouse or any person under age 18 within the past two years. Joint custody may be granted after the judge considers: (1) if joint custody will benefit child's physical, psychological, and emotional needs and development; (2) ability of parties to give child first priority and reach shared decisions; (3) ability to encourage relationship between the child and other parent; (4) whether both parents participated in rearing the child before filing; (5) geographical proximity of the parent's homes; (6) preferences of the child if at least 12 years of age; and, (7) any other relevant factor.

(continued)

Child Support

If payor's monthly net resources are under $6000, then a percentage of monthly net resources as follows: 20% for one child, 25% for two children, 30% for three children, 35% for four children, 40% for five children, and over 40% for six or more children. If net resources are over $6000, then may order additional child support. Termination age: 18.

Termination of Parental Rights

Grounds: (1) danger to physical health or safety by parent; (2) abuse or neglect; and, (3) sexual abuse of another child by the parent.

Utah

The Law	Utah Code Annotated 1953.
	Example: Utah Code, Title 30, Chapter 3, Section 30-3-1 (U.C. Sec. 30-3-1).
Case Style	IN THE DISTRICT COURT OF THE _____ JUDICIAL DISTRICT [each district has a number], IN AND FOR _____ COUNTY, STATE OF UTAH
Designation of Parties	_____, Plaintiff, vs. _____, Defendant.
Custody	Best interest of the child considering: (1) past conduct and demonstrated moral standards of the parties; (2) child's wishes; (3) which party is most likely to act in the child's best interest, including allowing contact with the other party; and, (4) any other relevant factor.
Child Support	State child support guidelines available at U.C. Sec. 78-45-7. Termination age: 18.
Termination of Parental Rights	Grounds: (1) abandonment; (2) neglect or abuse; and, (3) parent unfit or incompetent.

Vermont

The Law

Vermont Statutes Annotated.
Example: Vermont Statutes Annotated, Title 15, Section 551 (15 V.S.A. Sec. 551). Ignore chapter numbers.

Case Style

STATE OF VERMONT, SUPERIOR COURT, _____ COUNTY

Designation of Parties

_____, Plaintiff, vs.
_____, Defendant.

Custody

Best interest of the child considering: (1) relationship of the child and each party, and each party's ability and disposition to provide love, affection, and guidance; (2) ability and disposition to provide food, clothing, medical care, other material needs, and a safe environment; (3) ability and disposition to meet the child's present and future developmental needs; (4) quality of the child's adjustment to present housing, school, and community, and potential effect of a change; (5) ability and disposition to foster a continuing relationship with the other party; (6) quality of the child's relationship with primary caregiver; (7) child's relationship to other significant persons; (8) ability and disposition of the parties to make joint decisions; and, (9) any evidence of abuse.

Child Support

State child support guidelines available from court clerk. Termination age: 18.

Termination of
Parental Rights

Grounds: (1) parent does not exercise parental responsibility for the child; (2) fails to support the child in accordance with financial means; (3) parent convicted of a crime of violence; and, (4) risk of substantial harm to physical or psychological well-being of child.

Virginia

The Law

Code of Virginia 1950.
Example: Code of Virginia, Title 20, Section 20-91 (C.V. Sec. 20-91). Ignore "chapter" numbers; look for "title" and "section" numbers.

Case Style

VIRGINIA: IN THE _____
COURT OF _____
[Call the clerk or look in a court file to see what should go in the blanks]

Designation of Parties

_____, Plaintiff, vs.
_____, Defendant.

Custody

Best interest of the child considering: (1) age, physical, and mental condition of the child and the parties; (2) relationship between the child and each party; (3) needs of child; (4) the role each party played and will play in the child's upbringing and care; (5) any history of family abuse; (6) propensity of each parent to support a relationship and contact with the child and the other parent; (7) child's preference if suitable age, intelligence, and understanding; and, (8) any other relevant factor.

Child Support

State child support guidelines can be found at C.V. Sec. 20-108.2. Termination age: 18.

Termination of
Parental Rights

Grounds: (1) mental and emotional illness or mental defect of parent; (2) habitual substance abuse by parent; and, (3) neglect or abuse of the child by the parent.

Washington

The Law	West's Revised Code of Washington Annotated. ***Example:*** Revised Code of Washington Annotated, Title 26, Chapter 26.09, Section 26.09.010 (R.C.W.A. Sec. 26.09.010).
Case Style	IN THE _____ COURT OF THE STATE OF WASHINGTON, IN AND FOR THE COUNTY OF _____ [depending upon the term used in your county, either the word "SUPERIOR" or "FAMILY" goes in the first blank]
Designation of Parties	_____, Petitioner, vs. _____, Respondent.
Custody	Factors: (1) each party's relative strength, nature, and stability of the relationship with the child including which party has taken greater responsibility for the child; (2) any agreement between the parties; (3) each party's past and potential for future performance of parenting functions; (4) child's emotional needs and development; (5) the child's relationship with siblings and other significant adults and involvement in his or her physical surroundings, school, and other activities; (6) the wishes of the parties and the child; and, (7) each party's employment schedule. The greatest weight is given to the first factor listed above.

Child Support

State child support guidelines can be found in Title 26, Chapter 26.19 of the Revised Code. Termination age: 18.

Termination of Parental Rights

Grounds: (1) habitual substance abuse by parent and (2) psychological incapacity or mental deficiency of parent.

West Virginia

The Law	West Virginia Code. **Example:** West Virginia Code, Chapter 48, Article 2, Section 48-2-1 (W.V.C. Sec. 48-2-1).
Case Style	CIRCUIT COURT OF _____ COUNTY, WEST VIRGINIA
Designation of Parties	_____, Plaintiff, vs. _____, Defendant.
Custody	No statutory factors. Presumption in favor of primary caretaker.
Child Support	Child support determined by dividing the total child support obligation between the parents in proportion to their income using their adjusted gross income. Termination age: 18.
Termination of Parental Rights	Grounds: (1) abandonment and (2) abuse or neglect.

Wisconsin

The Law	West's Wisconsin Statutes Annotated. **Example:** Wisconsin Statutes Annotated, Section 767.001 (W.S.A. Sec. 767.001). Ignore "chapter" numbers.
Case Style	STATE OF WISCONSIN: CIRCUIT COURT, _____ COUNTY
Designation of Parties	_____, Petitioner, vs. _____, Respondent.
Custody	Referred to as "legal custody and physical placement." Best interest of the child considering: (1) wishes of parties; (2) wishes of child; (3) interaction and inter-relationship between child and the parties, siblings, and any other significant person; (4) child's adjustment to home, school, and community; (5) mental and physical health of all parties involved; (6) availability of public and private child care services; (7) whether one is likely to unreasonably interfere with child's continuing relationship with the other party; (8) any evidence of child abuse; (9) any evidence of domestic abuse; (9) whether either party has had a significant problem with alcohol or drug abuse; and, (11) any other relevant factor.

(continued)

Child Support   Child support determined by formula,
                                 with 17% of gross income awarded for
                                 one child, 25% for two children, 29% for
                                 three children, and 34% for five or more
                                 children. This may be reduced according
                                 to the amount of time the payor spends
                                 with the child. Termination age: 18.

Termination of   Grounds: (1) abandonment; (2) continuing
Parental Rights   need of protection or services; (3) con-
                                 tinuing parental responsibility; (4) child
                                 abuse; (5) failure to assume parental
                                 responsibility; (6) incestuous parent-
                                 hood; and, (7) intentional killing of
                                 opposing parent.

Wyoming

The Law	Wyoming Statutes Annotated. ***Example:*** Wyoming Statutes Annotated, Title 20, Chapter 2, Section 20-2-104 (W.S.A. Sec. 20-2-104).
Case Style	IN THE DISTRICT COURT IN AND FOR _____ COUNTY, WYOMING
Designation of Parties	_____, Plaintiff, vs. _____, Defendant.
Custody	Custody to be determined "as appears most expedient and beneficial for the well-being of the children. The court shall consider the relative competency of both parents and no award of custody shall be made solely on the basis of gender of parent."
Child Support	Factors: (1) age of child; (2) cost of necessary child day care; (3) special health care and educational needs of the child; (4) expenses reasonable related to the mother's pregnancy if the parents were never married; (5) cost of transportation of the child to and from visitation; and, (6) amount of time the child spends with each parent. Termination age: 18.
Termination of Parental Rights	Grounds: (1) abandonment; (2) neglect or abuse; and, (3) parental incarceration and unfitness.

APPENDIX B:
SAMPLE FORMS

This appendix contains sample forms that are typical of those used in most states. However, because each state is different (and sometimes each county is different), you will need to do some research to be sure your forms will be accepted by the courts in your state and county. Before following the forms in this appendix, be sure you:

 ♦ read the information for your state in Appendix A of this book;
 ♦ check with your clerk of court to find out if there are any official forms you can or must use. If so, use the official forms; and,
 ♦ review one or more court files of the type of case you will be filing at your court clerk's office to see how papers are prepared in your area, then use the same format.

The sample forms in this appendix have been completed based upon the following information for a fictional state.

SUPERIOR

The Law: Superior Statutes Annotated.
           Example: Superior Statutes Annotated, Title 40, Chapter 1, Section 40-1-101 (S.S.A. Sec. 40-1-101).

Case Style: IN THE _____ CIRCUIT COURT, IN
           AND FOR _____ COUNTY,
           SUPERIOR

Designation   _____, Plaintiff, and _____, Defendant.
of Parties:

Custody:	Best interest of the child, considering: (1) age and sex of child; (2) wishes of parents and child; (3) interaction and interrelationship between the child and parents, siblings, and other significant persons; and, (4) mental and physical health of all persons involved.
Child Support:	Child support guidelines found in S.S.A. Sec. 40-4-130. Termination age: 18.
Termination of Parental Rights:	Grounds: (1) abandonment; (2) emotional or mental illness or mental deficiency of parent; (3) excessive substance abuse by parent; (4) child abused or neglected, or in danger of abuse, by parent; or, (5) parent convicted and imprisoned for felony.

Table of Forms

IN THE FIFTH CIRCUIT COURT, IN AND FOR COLUMBIA COUNTY, SUPERIOR

Jane Doe,
        Plaintiff,

vs.   CASE NO: _____

John Smith,
        Defendant.

COMPLAINT FOR PATERNITY

Plaintiff alleges the following:

1. This is an action seeking the establishment of paternity pursuant to __S.S.A., Section 42-2-101_____.

2. The Plaintiff is a citizen and resident of __Columbia County Superior_____. Based upon information and belief, Plaintiff alleges that the Defendant is a citizen and resident of _____Columbia County, Superior_____.

3. The minor child named _____Veronica Doe_____, was born on __February 14, 2006__, in ____Columbia____ County, _____Superior_____.

4. The Plaintiff is the minor child's biological mother.

5. The Plaintiff believes that the Defendant is the minor child's biological father based upon the following facts and circumstances:

☒   a.   At the time of both conception and delivery of the minor child, the Plaintiff was not married to the Defendant nor married to anyone else.

☒   b.   The Plaintiff and Defendant had sexual relations during the months preceding the birth of the child.

☒   c.   Other: <u>The Plaintiff has blood type A,</u>
<u>the minor child has blood type O, and</u>
<u>the Defendant has informed the</u>
<u>Plaintiff that he has blood type O.</u>

6. There are no custody or visitation actions with respect to the minor child which are currently pending.

7. Inasmuch as a question as to the parentage of the minor child has arisen in this action, Plaintiff moves the Court for entry of an order directing that Plaintiff, Defendant, and the minor child submit to genetic testing, HLA blood testing, and/or other appropriate blood tests and comparisons which have been developed and adapted for purposes of establishing or disproving parentage and which are reasonably accessible to the parties involved.

Wherefore, Plaintiff prays the Court as follows:

1. That the Court enter an Order directing that Plaintiff and Defendant and the minor child named above submit to genetic testing, HLA blood testing, and/or any other tests and comparison which have been developed and adapted for the purposes of establishing or disproving parentage and which are reasonably assessable to the parties involved.

2. That this verified complaint be taken as an affidavit upon which upon which the Court can base all of its orders in this case.

3. That the costs of this action be taxed to the ~~Plaintiff~~ / Defendant.

4. That the Court grant to Plaintiff such other and further relief as may be just and proper.

This <u>16th</u> day of <u>March</u>, <u>2006</u>.

<u>Jane Doe</u>

Pro Se

Name: <u>Jane Doe</u>
Address: <u>127 Walnut Street</u>
<u>Superior City, SU 99999</u>
Telephone: <u>(222) 555-5155</u>

IN THE FIFTH CIRCUIT COURT, IN AND FOR
COLUMBIA COUNTY, SUPERIOR

Jane Doe,
    Plaintiff,

vs.   CASE NO: _____

John Smith,
    Defendant.

COMPLAINT FOR CUSTODY

Plaintiff / ~~Petitioner~~ alleges the following:

1. This is an action seeking temporary and permanent custody of a minor child(~~ren~~), pursuant to <u>S.S.A., Section 42-3-105</u>.

2. The Plaintiff / ~~Petitioner~~ is a citizen and resident of <u>Columbia County, Superior</u>. Based upon information and belief, Plaintiff /~~xPetitioner~~ alleges that the Defendant / ~~Respondent~~ is a citizen and resident of <u>Columbia County, Superior</u>

<u>   </u>.

3. The Plaintiff / ~~Petitioner~~ is the _____<u>mother</u>_____ of the minor child(~~ren~~): <u>Veronica Doe</u>, born <u>February 14, 2006</u>

<u>   </u> ~~respectively~~.

4. The Defendant / ~~Respondent~~ is the minor child(~~ren~~)'s <u>father</u>.

5. Plaintiff /~~xPetitioner~~ is a fit and proper person to have the general care, custody, and control of the minor child(~~ren~~).

6. It is in the best interest of the minor child(~~ren~~) that custody be awarded to the Plaintiff / ~~Petitioner~~

WHEREFORE, Plaintiff / ~~Petitioner~~ prays the court for relief as follows:

1. That the foregoing Complaint / ~~Petition~~ be accepted as an affidavit in support of the Plaintiff's / ~~Petitioner's~~ application for both temporary and permanent custody of the minor child(~~ren~~), and that said Complaint / ~~Petition~~ also be allowed and taken as an affidavit upon which to base all orders of the Court.

2. That an order be entered herein awarding the temporary and permanent custody of the minor child(~~ren~~) to the Plaintiff / ~~Petitioner~~

3. That the Court grant such other and further relief as it deems just and proper.

This ___16th___ day of _____March_____, ____2006__.

_____*Jane Doe*_____

Pro Se

Name:_____Jane Doe_____

Address: ___127 Walnut Street_____

_____Superior City, SU 99999____

Telephone: __(222) 555-5155_____

IN THE FIFTH CIRCUIT COURT, IN AND FOR
COLUMBIA COUNTY, SUPERIOR

John Smith,
    Petitioner,

vs.   CASE NO: _____

Jane Doe,
    Respondent.

PETITION FOR VISITATION

~~Plaintiff~~ / Petitioner alleges the following:

1. This is an action seeking visitation with a minor child(~~ren~~), pursuant to __S.S.A., Section 42-3-105__.

2. The ~~Plaintiff~~ / Petitioner is a citizen and resident of __Columbia County, Superior__. Based upon information and belief, ~~Plaintiff~~/ Petitioner alleges that the ~~Defendant~~ / Respondent is a citizen and resident of __Columbia County, Superior__ _____.

3. The ~~Plaintiff~~/ Petitioner is the __father__ of the minor child(~~ren~~): __Veronica Doe__ _____, born __February 14, 2006__ _____ ~~respectively~~.

4. The ~~Defendant~~ / Respondent is the minor child(~~ren~~)'s __mother__.

5. ~~Plaintiff~~/ Petitioner is a fit and proper person to have visitation privileges with the minor child(~~ren~~).

6. It is in the best interest of the minor child(~~ren~~) that visitation privileges be awarded to the ~~Plaintiff~~/ Petitioner.

WHEREFORE, ~~Plaintiff~~ / Petitioner prays the court for relief as follows:

1. That the foregoing ~~Complaint~~ / Petition be accepted as an affidavit in support of the ~~Plaintiff's~~ / Petitioner's application for visitation with the minor child(~~ren~~), and that said ~~Complaint~~ / Petition also be allowed and taken as an affidavit upon which to base all orders of the Court.

2. That an order be entered awarding the following visitation privileges to the ~~Plaintiff~~/ Petitioner.

```
Alternate weekends from 7:00 p.m. Friday until
4:00 p.m. Sunday; alternating holidays of New
Years Day, Easter, Memorial Day, Fourth of July,
Labor Day, Thanksgiving Day, Christmas Eve, and
Christmas Day; every Father's Day; and, one week
during summer vacation from school.
```

3. That the Court grant such other and further relief as it deems just and proper.

This <u>16th</u> day of <u>March</u>, <u>2006</u>.

<u>*John Smith*</u>

Pro Se

Name: <u>John Smith</u>

Address: <u>1482 Lakeshore Drive</u>

<u>Superior City, SU 99999</u>

Telephone: <u>(222) 555-5555</u>

IN THE FIFTH CIRCUIT COURT, IN AND FOR
COLUMBIA COUNTY, SUPERIOR

Jane Doe,
      Plaintiff,

vs.   CASE NO: _____

John Smith,
      Defendant.

CHILD SUPPORT COMPLAINT

Plaintiff / ~~Petitioner~~ alleges the following:

1. This is an action seeking child support on behalf of a minor child(~~ren~~), pursuant to __S.S.A., Section 42-3-106__ .

2. The Plaintiff / ~~Petitioner~~ is a citizen and resident of __Columbia County, SU__ . Based upon information and belief, Plaintiff / ~~Petitioner~~ alleges that the Defendant / ~~Respondent~~ is a citizen and resident of __Columbia County, SU__ .

3. The Plaintiff / ~~Petitioner~~ is the __mother__ of the minor child(~~ren~~): __Veronica Doe__ _____ , born __February 14, 2006__ _____ ~~respectively~~.

4. The Defendant / ~~Respondent~~ is the minor child(~~ren~~)'s __father__ .

5. The minor child(~~ren~~) has/have been in the actual physical custody of the Plaintiff / ~~Petitioner~~ since __February 14, 2006__

6. The Defendant / ~~Respondent~~ is able-bodied and capable of providing financial support on behalf of the minor child(~~ren~~). He/~~she~~ is employed at __Superior Auto Repair__ and earns approximately $ __26,000.00__ per year.

7. The minor child(~~ren~~) is in need of support.

8. The minor child(~~ren~~) ___has/have _X_ has no/~~have no~~ extraordinary expenses.

WHEREFORE, Plaintiff / Petitioner prays the court for relief as follows:

1. That the foregoing Complaint / Petition be accepted as an affidavit in support of the Plaintiff's / Petitioner's application for child support and that this Complaint / Petition also be allowed and taken as an affidavit upon which to base all orders of the Court.

2. That an order be entered directing the Defendant / Respondent to pay child support pursuant to the child support guidelines.

3. That the Court grant such other and further relief as it deems just and proper.

This __16th__ day of _____March_____, ____2006__.

_____*Jane Doe*_____

                                                    Pro Se

Name:__ Jane Doe _____

Address: 127 Walnut Street _____

_____ Superior City, SU 99999 _____

Telephone: _(222) 555-5155_____

IN THE FIFTH CIRCUIT COURT, IN AND FOR
COLUMBIA COUNTY, SUPERIOR

Jane Doe,
     Petitioner,

vs.   CASE NO: _____

John Smith,
     Respondent.

PETITION TO TERMINATE PARENTAL RIGHTS

The Petitioner alleges the following:

1. This is an action seeking the termination of the parental rights of the Respondent pursuant to <u>S.S.A., </u>_____
<u>Section 102-1-201</u>_____.

2. The name(s) of the minor child(ren) who is/are the subject of this petition is/are: <u>Veronica Doe</u>
_____,
born <u>February 14, 2006</u>_____
_____ respectively.

3. The Respondent is the biological father of the minor child(ren) and is believed to reside in <u>Columbia County, Superior</u>
_____.

4. The Petitioner is the biological mother of the minor child(ren); and resides in <u>Columbia County, Superior</u>
_____ and has so resided there with the minor child(ren) since _____
<u>February 16,</u>_____, <u>2006</u>.

5. The Petitioner and the Respondent were never married and the Petitioner has had the actual physical custody of the minor child(ren) since _____<u>February 14,</u>_____, <u>2006</u>_____.

6. ☒   No person has been appointed as guardian ad litem for the minor child(~~ren~~) in this or any other action.

  ❑

         _____

         has been appointed as guardian ad litem for the minor child(ren) in this action.

7. The parental rights of the Respondent are subject to termination because:

The Respondent has abandoned the minor child, by
failing to provide any financial support and failing
to make any attempt to contact the minor child since
the child's birth.

_____

_____

8. This petition has not been filed to circumvent any provisions of the Uniform Child Custody Jurisdiction Act.

WHEREFORE, the Petitioner prays that the parental rights of the Respondent be terminated.

This __16th__ day of __March__ , __2006__ .

_____ *Jane Doe* _____

                                               Pro Se

Name: __Jane Doe__

Address: __127 Walnut Street__

__Superior City, SU 99999__

Telephone: __(222) 555-5155__

VERIFICATION

I, _____Jane Doe_____ being first duly
sworn, depose and say:

That I am the Plaintiff in this action;

That I have read the foregoing ___ Complaint _X_ Petition ___ Motion
and know the contents thereof;

That the same is true of my own knowledge, save and except those
matters and things therein stated upon information and belief, and
as to those matters and things, I believe them to be true.

This _16th_ day of _____March_____, ___2006__.

_____*Jane Doe*_____
                                                      Affiant

STATE OF _____
COUNTY OF _____
Sworn to and subscribed before me this _____ day
of _____, _____.

_____
Notary Public
My Commission Expires: _____

IN THE FIFTH CIRCUIT COURT, IN AND FOR
COLUMBIA COUNTY, SUPERIOR

Jane Doe,
  Plaintiff,

vs.   CASE NO: _____

John Smith,
  Defendant.

UNIFORM CHILD CUSTODY JURISDICTION ACT AFFIDAVIT

1. The name and present address of each child (under 18) in this case is:
  Veronica Doe
  127 Walnut Street
  Superior City, SU 99999

2. The places where the child(ren) has/have lived within the last five years are:
  127 Walnut Street
  Superior City, SU 99999

3. The name(s) and present address(es) of custodians with whom the child(ren) has/have lived within the past five years are:
  Jane Doe
  127 Walnut Street
  Superior City, SU 99999

4. I do not know of and have not participated (as a party, witness, or in any other capacity) in any other court decision, order, or proceeding (including divorce, separate maintenance, child neglect, dependency, or guardianship) concerning the custody or visitation of the child(ren) in this state or any other state, except: [Specify case name and number and court's name and address.]
  none

5. I do not have information of any proceeding (including divorce, separate maintenance, child neglect, dependency, or guardianship) concerning the custody or visitation of the child(ren), in this state or any other state except: [specify case name and number and court's name and address.]

    none

That proceeding ___ is continuing ___ has been stayed by the court.

___ Temporary action by this court is necessary to protect the child(ren) because the child(ren) has/have been subjected to or threatened with mistreatment or abuse or is/are otherwise neglected or dependent.

[Attach explanation.]

6. I do not know of any person who is not already a party to this proceeding who has physical custody of, or who claims to have custody or visitation rights with, the child(ren), except: [state name(s) and address(es).]

    none

7. The child(ren)'s "home state" is ___Superior_____
["Home State" means the state in which the child(ren), immediately preceding the time involved, lived with his or her parents, a parent, or a person acting as a parent, for at least six consecutive months, and, in the case of a child less than six months old, the state in which the child lived from birth with any of the persons mentioned. Periods of temporary absence of the named persons are counted as a part of the six month or other period.]

I acknowledge a continuing duty to advise this court of any custody or visitation proceeding (including dissolution of marriage, separate maintenance, child neglect, or dependent) concerning the child(ren) in this state or any other state about which information is obtained during this proceeding.

This ___16th___ day of _____March_____, __2006__.

_____*Jane Doe*_____
Signature of Affiant

Name_____Jane Doe_____

Address ___127 Walnut Street_____

_____Superior City, SU 99999_____

Telephone No. ___(222) 555-5155___

STATE OF _____

COUNTY OF _____

Sworn to and subscribed before me this _____ day of _____, _____.

_____

Notary Public

My Commission Expires: _____

IN THE FIFTH CIRCUIT COURT, IN AND FOR
COLUMBIA COUNTY, SUPERIOR

Jane Doe,
    Plaintiff,

vs.   CASE NO: __03-421__

John Smith,
    Defendant.

ANSWER

Defendant / ~~Respondent~~, answering the allegations of the Plaintiff / ~~Petitioner~~, alleges the following:

1. The allegations contained in paragraphs __1 through 3__ _____ of the __Child Support Complaint__ are true and correct.

2. The allegations contained in paragraphs __4 through 8__ _____ are denied.

WHEREFORE, Defendant / ~~Respondent~~ prays the court for relief as follows:

1. That the foregoing Answer be allowed and taken as an affidavit upon which to base all orders of the Court.

2. That an order be entered _____ __dismissing the Child Support Complaint__ _____.

3. That the Court grant such other and further relief as it deems just and proper.

This __29th__ day of _____March_____, __2006__.

_____*John Smith*_____
                        Pro Se

Name___John Smith___
Address___1482 Lakeshore Dr.___
_____Superior City, SU   99999___
Telephone No. _222-555-5555_

IN THE FIFTH CIRCUIT COURT, IN AND FOR
COLUMBIA COUNTY, SUPERIOR

Jane Doe,
  Plaintiff,

vs.   CASE NO: _____

John Smith,
  Defendant.

SUMMONS

TO: Each Sheriff of the State of <u>Superior</u>   .

YOU ARE COMMANDED to serve this Summons and a copy of
the Complaint / ~~Petition~~ in this action on the Defendant(s) /
~~Respondent(s)~~):
    John Smith
    1482 Lakeshore Drive
    Superior City, SU 99999

The Defendant(s) / ~~Respondent(s)~~ is /~~are~~ required to serve written
defenses to the Complaint / ~~Petition~~ on the Plaintiff(s) /
~~Petitioner(s)~~ Jane Doe
    127 Walnut Street
    Superior City, SU 99999

within <u> 20 </u> calendar days after this Summons is served on the
Defendant(s) / ~~Respondent(s)~~ exclusive of the day of service, and
to file the original of the defenses with the clerk of this court either
before service on the Plaintiff(s) / ~~Petitioner(s)~~ or immediately
thereafter.

If any Defendant / R̶e̶s̶p̶o̶n̶d̶e̶n̶t̶ fails to serve and file defenses as
stated above, a default may be entered against the Defendant /
R̶e̶s̶p̶o̶n̶d̶e̶n̶t̶ for the relief demanded in the Complaint / P̶e̶t̶i̶t̶i̶o̶n̶

This __16th__ day of ____March____, __2006__ .

CLERK OF THE COURT

By:_____

IN THE FIFTH CIRCUIT COURT, IN AND FOR
COLUMBIA COUNTY, SUPERIOR

Jane Doe,
       Plaintiff,

vs.   CASE NO: __06-421__

John Smith,
       Defendant.

CERTIFICATE OF SERVICE

I, _____Jane Doe_____,
certify that a copy of the __Plaintiff's Financial__
__Affidavit_____ was served upon the opposing
party or his/her attorney by depositing a copy of the same in
the United States mail with prepaid, first-class postage, and
addressed as follows: John Smith
                      1482 Lakeshore Dr.
                      Superior City, SU 99999
This __19th___ day of ____March_____, __2006___.

_____*Jane Doe*_____
       Name: ___Jane Doe_____
       Address: __127 Walnut Street_____
       _____Superior City, SU 99999___
       Telephone: _222-555-5155_____

IN THE FIFTH CIRCUIT COURT, IN AND FOR
COLUMBIA COUNTY, SUPERIOR

Jane Doe,
     Plaintiff,

vs.   CASE NO: 06-421

John Smith,
     Defendant.

NOTICE OF HEARING

To: John Smith

PLEASE TAKE NOTICE that the Child Support Complaint
will be called for hearing on Friday, the 21st
day of April, 2006, at 9:00 A.M., before
the Honorable Barry D. Hatchett, Judge of
the above-titled court, at Room 245, Columbia County
Courthouse, 12 Main Street, Superior City, SU 99999.

Jane Doe
                                    Signature

Name: Jane Doe
Address: 127 Walnut Street
              Superior City, SU 99999
Telephone: 222-555-5155

IN THE FIFTH CIRCUIT COURT, IN AND FOR
COLUMBIA COUNTY, SUPERIOR

Jane Doe,
        Plaintiff,

vs.   CASE NO: __06-421__

John Smith,
        Defendant.

SUBPOENA

TO: Payroll Clerk
      Superior Auto Repair
      42918 24th Street
      Superior, SU 99999

YOU ARE HEREBY COMMANDED to appear before the
Honorable Barry D. Hatchett _____,
Judge of the Court, at __Room 245, Columbia County__
__Courthouse, 12 Main Street, Superior City, SU 99999__,
on __Friday__, __April 21__, __2006__, at
__9:00__ o'clock __A__. M., to:

[check all that apply]

☒ testify in the above-entitled action.
☒ produce the following items:

IF YOU FAIL TO APPEAR,
YOU MAY BE IN CONTEMPT OF COURT.

You are subpoenaed to appear by the attorney or party designated below, and unless excused from this subpoena by said attorney or party, or by the court, you shall respond to this subpoena as directed.

If you have any questions about being subpoenaed as a witness, you should contact the attorney or party listed below who had the subpoena issued

This ___12th___ day of _____April_____, ___2006___.

CLERK OF THE COURT

By:_____

Attorney or Party Requesting Subpoena:

Name:___Jane Doe_____

Address: ___127 Walnut Street_____

_____Superior City, SU 99999_____

Telephone No.___222-555-5155_____

IN THE FIFTH CIRCUIT COURT, IN AND FOR
COLUMBIA COUNTY, SUPERIOR

Jane Doe,
      Plaintiff,

vs.   CASE NO: _06-2306_____

John Smith,
      Defendant.

JUDGMENT OF PATERNITY

This matter coming on to be heard and being heard before the undersigned Judge of the ___Circuit Court_____, ___Columbia_____ County, ___Superior_____, on the _12th_ day of ___May_____, _2006_, upon the ___Complaint for Paternity_____ filed in the above-entitled action;

And it appearing to the Court that the Plaintiff / ~~Petitioner~~ was present in court and proceeding pro se and that the Defendant / ~~Respondent~~ was in court and proceeding pro se / ~~represented by legal counsel~~

Upon hearing testimony herein and upon considering the verified pleading of the Plaintiff / ~~Petitioner~~, matters contained in the court file and other evidence introduced by the parties, the Court makes and enters the following:

FINDINGS OF FACT AND CONCLUSIONS OF LAW

1. All parties are properly before the Court and the Court has jurisdiction over the parties and the subject matter.

2. The Plaintiff / ~~Petitioner~~ is a citizen and resident of ___Columbia_____ County, ___Superior_____.

3. The Defendant / ~~Respondent~~ is a citizen and resident of ___Columbia_____ County, ___Superior_____.

251

4. Based upon the results of scientific testing, and other evidence presented at hearing, the parties are the biological parents of ___1___ minor child(ren): __Veronica Doe__

_____,
born on ___February 14, 2006_____ ~~respectively~~

5. The [Plaintiff / ~~Petitioner] [Defendant /Respondent~~] is a fit and proper person to have the care, custody, and control of the minor child(ren) and it is in the child(ren)'s best interest to award the Plaintiff / ~~Petitioner~~ custody.

6. The ~~[Plaintiff / Petitioner]~~ [Defendant /~~Respondent~~] is a fit and proper person to have visitation privileges with the minor child(ren) and it is in the child(ren)'s best interest to award the ~~[Plaintiff / Petitioner]~~ [Defendant /~~Respondent~~] visitation privileges.

7. The ~~[Plaintiff / Petitioner]~~ [Defendant / ~~Respondent~~] is financially able to contribute the sum of $___250.00____ per ___week_____ to the support or the minor child(ren).

IT IS THEREFORE ORDERED, ADJUDGED, AND DECREED THAT:

1. The ~~[Plaintiff / Petitioner]~~ [Defendant /~~Respondent~~] be declared to be the biological father of the minor child(ren).

2. The [Plaintiff / ~~Petitioner] [Defendant / Respondent~~] be awarded the care, custody, and control of the minor child(ren).

3. The ~~[Plaintiff / Petitioner]~~ [Defendant / ~~Respondent~~] be awarded visitation with the minor child(ren) as follows:

Alternate weekends from 7:00 p.m. Friday until 4:00 p.m. Sunday; alternating holidays of New Years Day, Easter,Memorial Day, Fourth of July, Labor Day, Thanksgiving Day, Christmas Eve, and Christmas Day; every Father's Day; and, one week during summer vacation from sf two-week's notice.

4. The ~~[Plaintiff / Petitioner]~~ [Defendant / ~~Respondent~~] shall pay the sum of $___250.00____ per ___week___ for the support and maintenance of the minor child(ren).

5. The Plaintiff / ~~Petitioner~~ and the Defendant / ~~Respondent~~ have an affirmative duty to maintain a suitable and proper environment for the minor child(~~ren~~) at such times as the child(~~ren~~) is/~~are~~ in their care.

6. Neither party shall permanently remove the minor child(~~ren~~) from the jurisdiction of this Court without the prior permission of this Court.

This __23rd__ day of ____May____, ____2006__.

Barry D. Hatchett
_____
                                                        Judge

CIVIL COVER SHEET

The civil cover sheet and the information contained herein neither replace nor supplement the filing and service of pleadings or other papers as required by law. This form is required for the use of the Clerk of Court for the purposes of reporting judicial workload data pursuant to section 21.005, Superior Statutes Annotated.

I. CASE STYLE

Jane Doe
Plaintiff / ~~Petitioner~~

Case No. _06-35678_

vs.

Division: _L_

John Smith
Defendant / ~~Respondent~~.

II. TYPE OF CASE

(Place an X in one box only. If the case fits more than one type of case, select the most definite.)

Domestic Relations

- ❏ Divorce
- ❏ Domestic Violence
- ☒ Paternity
- ❏ Child Support
- ❏ Custody
- ❏ Visitation
- ❏ Other domestic relations

Torts

- ❏ Professional Malpractice
- ❏ Products Liability
- ❏ Auto Negligence
- ❏ Other Negligence

Other Civil

- ❏ Contracts
- ❏ Real Property/
- ❏ Mortgage Foreclosure
- ❏ Eminent Domain
- ❏ Other

III. IS JURY TRIAL DEMANDED IN COMPLAINT?

❏ Yes   ☒ No

DATE March 20, 2006

Jane Doe

SIGNATURE OF ATTORNEY OR PARTY
INITIATING ACTION:

Name: Jane Doe
Address: 127 Walnut Street
Superior City, SU 99999
Phone: 222-555-5155

APPENDIX C:
RESOURCES

WEBSITES

About.com Single Parents
http://singleparents.about.com

Air Force Family Separation and Readiness
www.afcrossroads.com/
famseparation/ret_parent.cfm

Celebrating Children: Single African American Parenting
www.celebratingchildren.com

Child Custody Organization
www.childcustody.org

Child Custody Resources
www.custody911.com

Child Custody: Single Parent Discussion Forum
www.winchildcustody.com/
singleparent

Dads at a Distance
www.daads.com

Discussion Board for Custodial Parents
www.mafiaboard.com/forum

Fathers Are Parents Too
www.fapt.org

Fathers Network
www.fathersnetwork.org

Federal Office of Child Support Enforcement
www.acf.dhhs.gov/programs/cse/
index.html

Grandparents' Visitation Rights
www.grandtimes.com/visit.html

Moms Over Miles
www.momsovermiles.com

National Adoption Information Clearinghouse
www.naic.acf.hhs.gov

Parenting Help
www.ceinfo.unh.edu/Family/Parent.htm

Parenting Monthly: Tips for Fathers
www.parentingmonthly.org/
dads_info.html

Parenting Teens
www.parentingteens.com

Parents Without Partners
www.parentswithoutpartners.org

Parents World
www.parentsworld.com

Paternity Information Page
www.peak.org/~jedwards/
paternity.html

Paternity Issues
www.vix.com/men/
child-support/paternity.html

Responsible Single Fathers
www.singlefather.org

Single Dads' Index
www.menweb.org/throop/
single-dad.html

Single Mothers Online
www.singlemothers.org

Single Parent Central
www.singleparentcentral.com/
index.htm

Single Parent Tips
http://singleparent.lifetips.com/
OurGurus.asp

Single Parents Network
www.singleparentsnetwork.com

Supervised Visitation Network
www.svnetwork.net

Unmarried Parents' Concerns
www.consumeraffairs.com/parenting/
unmarried.html

Youth Behavioral Issues
www.notmykid.org

ORGANIZATIONS

**Alliance for Non-Custodial
Parents' Rights**
www.ancpr.org

Alternatives to Marriage Project
P.O. Box 1922
Albany, NY 12201
518-462-5600
www.unmarried.org

**American Coalition for Fathers
and Children**
1718 Main Street N.W.
Suite 187
Washington, DC 20036
800-978-DADS
www.acfc.org

Children's Rights Council
6200 Editors Park Drive
Suite 103
Hyattsville, MD 20782
301-559-3120
www.gocrc.com

**National Center for Missing and
Exploited Children (NCMEC)**
Charles B. Wang International
Children's Building
699 Prince Street
Alexandria, VA 22314-3175
800-THE-LOST
(800-843-5678)
703-274-3900
www.missingkids.com

**National Clearinghouse for
Alcohol and Drug Information
(NCADI)**
P.O. Box 2345
Rockville, MD 20847-2345
301-468-2600
800-729-6686
www.health.org

**National Clearinghouse on Child
Abuse and Neglect Information**
Administration for Children and
Families
370 L'Enfant Promenade, S.W.
Washington, DC 20201
800-FYI-3366
703-385-7565
nccanch@calib.com
http://nccanch.acf.hhs.gov

Parents Anonymous
675 West Foothill Boulevard
Suite 220
Claremont, CA 91711-3475
909-621-6184
www.parentsanonymous.org

Parents Without Partners
1650 South Dixie Highway
Suite 510
Boca Raton, FL 33432
561-391-8833
www.parentswithoutpartners.org

Single and Custodial Father's Network, Inc.
608 Hastings Road
Pittsburgh, PA 15206
412-853-9903
www.scfn.org

Single Parents Association
4727 East Bell Road
Suite 45
PMB 209
Phoenix, AZ 85032
623-581-7445
www.singleparents.org

Unmarried America
P.O. Box 11030
Glendale, CA 91226
818-230-5156
www.unmarriedamerica.org

GENETIC TESTING LABORATORIES

American Red Cross Blood Services
Badger-Hawkeye Region
Parentage Laboratory
4880 Sheboygan Avenue
Madison, WI 53705
608-227-1239

Analytical Genetic Testing Center, Inc.
7808 Cherry Creek Drive South
#201
Denver, CO 80231
303-750-2023

Applied Genetics, Inc.
201 Summit View Drive
Suite 100
Brentwood, TN 37027
615-889-0444

Baltimore RH Typing Laboratory
400 West Franklin Street
Baltimore, MD 21201
410-225-9595

Blood Bank of San Bernardino and Riverside Counties
399 Blood Bank Road
San Bernardino, CA 92408
714-885-6503

Blood Center of Southeastern Wisconsin
638 North 18th Street
P.O. Box 2178
Milwaukee, WI 53201-2178
414-937-6206

Brotman Medical Center Blood Bank
3828 Delmas Terrace
Culver City, CA 90230
213-836-7000 x2350

Chinatown Medical Laboratory, Inc.
1239 Stockton Street
San Francisco, CA 94133
415-956-5481

Clinical Genetics Center
Specialty Diagnostics, Inc.
14241 East Imperial Highway
#C
La Mirada, CA 90638
213-941-6796

Clinical Testing and Research
20 Wilsey Square
Ridgewood, NJ 07450
201-652-2088

Fairfax Identity Laboratories
3025 Hamaker Court
Suite 203
Fairfax, VA 22031
800-848-4362
800-482-3025

Fong Diagnostic Laboratory
7237 East Southgate Drive
Suite 37
Sacramento, CA 95823
916-421-4167

Gene Prints
P.O. Box 278
Seal Beach, CA 90740
213-594-5947

Gene Proof Technologies
187 Graylynn Drive
Nashville, TN 37214
800-844-7851

Genetic Profiles Corporation
1060 Joshua Way
Vista, CA 92083
800-551-7763

GeneScreen
7237 East Southgate Drive
Sacramento, CA 95823
800-734-3664
GeneScreen, Inc.
2600 Stemmons Freeway
Suite 133
Dallas, TX 75207
800-362-8378

GeneScreen, Inc.
5698 Springboro Pike
Dayton, OH 45449
800-362-8378

Genetics and IVF Institute
3025 Hamaker Court
Suite 203
Fairfax, VA 22031
800-848-4362

Genetic Design, Inc.
7019 Albert Pick Road
Suite H
Greensboro, NC 27409
800-247-9540

Gentrix, Inc.
1350 South Loop Road
Suite 100
Alameda, CA 94501

Great Lakes Laboratories
118 East 8th Street
Michigan City, IN 46360
800-223-4549

Identity Genetics, Inc.
801 32nd Avenue
Brookings, SD 57006
800-861-1054

Immunological Association of Denver
717 Yosemite Circle
Denver, CO 80206-0351
303-365-9000

Indiana University Medical Genetics Services, Inc.
975 West Walnut Street
1B-130
Indianapolis, IN 46202-5251
317-274-1075

Irvin Memorial Blood Center
Scientific Services
270 Masonic Avenue
San Francisco, CA 94118
415-567-7400 x448

LabCorp, Inc.
P.O. Box 2200
1440 York Court Extension
Burlington, NC 27215
800-334-5161

LabCorp, Inc.
P.O. Box 2230
Burlington, NC 27216-2230
800-743-3944

Laboratory Corporation of America
1500 Caton Center Drive
Suite N
Arbutus, MD 21227
410-876-6959

Laboratory Corporation of America
1330 York Court Extension
Burlington, NC 27215
800-742-3944 x7416

LifeCodes
1400 Donelson Pike
Suite A
Nashville, TN 37217
615-360-5000

LifeCodes East Lansing Division
2248 Mt. Hope
Okemos, MI 48864
517-349-3890

Long Beach Genetics
San Jacinto Center
Austin, TX 78707
800-824-2699

Long Beach Genetics
201 Summit View Drive
#100
Brentwood, TN 37027
800-844-7851

Long Beach Genetics/Esoterix, Inc.
2384 East Pacifica Place
Rancho Dominquez, CA 90220
800-824-2699

Madera Community Hospital Laboratory
1250 East Almond Avenue
Madera, CA 93637
209-673-4485

Memorial Blood Centers of Minnesota, Inc.
2304 Park Avenue
Minneapolis, MN 55404-3789
800-982-9134

Memorial Medical Center of Long Beach
2801 Atlantic Avenue
Long Beach, CA 90806
213-595-3943

Micro Diagnostics
1400 Donelson Pike
Suite A15
Nashville, TN 37217
888-256-6383

Molecular Pathology Laboratory
424 East Church Avenue
Maryville, TN 37804
800-932-2943

National Legal Laboratories, Inc.
2947 Eyde Parkway
East Lansing, MI 48823
800-837-1504

National Legal Laboratories, Inc.
2248 East Mount Hope
Okemos, MI 48864
800-837-1504

Paternity Testing Corporation
3501 Berrywood Drive
Columbia, MO 65201

Pathological and Clinical Services
2111 East Dakota Avenue
P.O. Box 11866
Fresno, CA 93775
209-226-3551

Reliagene Technologies, Inc.
5525 Mounes Street
Suite 101
New Orleans, LA 70123
800-256-4106

Roberts Medical Group Laboratory
1808 Verdugo Boulevard
Glendale, CA 92108
818-790-4188

Roche Biomedical Laboratories
1447 York Court
Burlington, NC 27215
800-334-5161

Sci Med Consultants
489 Knickerbocker Road
Tenafly, NJ 07670

UC San Francisco
Immunogenetics Laboratory
Room HSE
520 Parnassus Avenue
San Francisco, CA 94143
415-476-3883

University of Puerto Rico
Pathology Department
HLA Laboratory
G.P.O. Box 29134
San Juan, PR 00929-0134

University of Utah Diagnostic
Laboratory
729 Arapeen Drive
Building 888
Room 150
Salt Lake City, UT 94108
801-585-3892

University of North Texas Health
Science Center
3500 Camp Bowie Boulevard
Fort Worth, TX 76107
800-687-5301

STATE-SPECIFIC RESICES
STATE-SPECIFIC
RESOURCES

ALABAMA
  Alabama Department of
  Human Resources
  Child Support Enforcement Division
  P.O. Box 304000
  Montgomery, AL 36130-4000
  334-242-9300
  Fax: 334-242-0606
  www.dhr.state.al.us

ALASKA
  Alaska Child Support
  Enforcement Division
  907-269-6900
  800-478-3300
  www.csed.state.ak.us

ARIZONA
  Arizona Department of
  Economic Security
  Division of Child Support
  Enforcement
  800-882-4151
  www.de.state.az.us

ARKANSAS
  Arkansas Department of Finance
  and Administration
  Office of Child Support
  Enforcement
  400 East Capitol
  P.O. Box 8133
  Little Rock, AR 72203
  501-682-6195
  Fax: 501-682-6002
  www.state.ar.us

CALIFORNIA
  California Department of Child
  Support Services
  P.O. Box 419064
  Rancho Cordova, CA 95741-9064
  866-249-0773
  Fax: 916-464-5065
  www.childsup.cahwnet.gov

COLORADO
  Colorado Department of
  Human Services
  Division of Child Support
  Enforcement
  1575 Sherman Street
  5th Floor
  Denver, CO 80203
  303-866-4300
  Fax: 303-866-4360
  www.childsupport.state.co.us

CONNECTICUT
Connecticut Department of
Social Services
25 Sigourney Street
Hartford, CT 06106-5033
800-842-1508
www.dss.state.ct.us

DELAWARE
Delaware Health and Social
Services
Division of Child Support
Enforcement
P.O. Box 904
84A Christiana Road
New Castle, DE 19720
302-577-7171
www.dhss.delaware.gov

DISTRICT OF COLUMBIA
Child Support
Enforcement Division
441 4th Street, N.W.
Suite 550 N
Washington, DC 20001
202-442-9900
www.csed.dc.gov

FLORIDA
Florida Child Support
Enforcement
800-622-KIDS (5437)
Dade County: 305-503-2740
Manatee: 941-741-4039
www.myflorida.com

GEORGIA
Office of Child Support
Enforcement
800-227-7993
404-463-8800
http://ocse.dhr.georgia.gov

HAWAII
Department of the
Attorney General
Child Support Enforcement Agency
888-317-9081
www.state.hi.us/csea

IDAHO
Department of
Health and Welfare
450 West State Street
10th Floor
P.O. Box 83720
Boise, ID 83720-0036
208-334-5500
www.healthandwelfare.idaho.gov

ILLINOIS
Illinois Department of Public Aid
Child Support Enforcement
Help Line: 800-447-4278
217-785-1692
www.illinois.gov

INDIANA
Indiana Family and Social
Services Administration
Child Support Bureau
P.O. Box 7083
402 West Washington Street
Indianapolis, IN 46207-7083
Child Support Hotline: 800-926-8332
www.in.gov

IOWA
Iowa Department of
Human Services
Hoover State Office Building
Des Moines, IA 50319
800-972-2017
www.dhs.state.ia.us

KANSAS
Kansas Department of Social and
Rehabilitation Services
Child Support Enforcement
915 Southwest Harrison Street
Topeka, KS 66612
785-296-3959
www.srskansas.org/cse

KENTUCKY
Office of the Attorney General
Child Support Enforcement
Commission
700 Capitol Avenue
Suite 126A
Frankfort, KY 40601
502-696-5675
http://ag.ky.gov

LOUISIANA
Department of Social Services
Child Support Enforcement Services
P.O. Box 94065
530 Lakeland Avenue
Baton Rouge, LA 70804-9065
225-342-4780
Fax: 225-342-7397
www.dss.state.la.us

MAINE
Department of Human Services
Division of Support Enforcement and
Recovery
11 SHS Whitten Road
Augusta, ME 04333
207-287-3110
Fax: 207-287-2334
www.state.me.us

MARYLAND
**Department of
Human Resources**
Child Support Enforcement
Administration
311 West Saratoga Street
Baltimore, MD 21201
800-925-4434
www.dhr.state.md.us

MASSACHUSETTS
**Child Support Enforcement
Division**
P.O. Box 7057
Boston, MA 02204
800-332-2733
www.state.ma.us/cse

MICHIGAN
Family Independence Agency
P.O. Box 30037
Lansing, MI 48909
517-373-2035
Fax: 517-335-6101
www.michigan.gov/fia

MINNESOTA
Department of Human Services
Child Support Enforcement
444 Lafayette Road
St. Paul, MN 55155-3846
651-296-2542
www.dhs.state.mn.us

MISSISSIPPI
**Mississippi Department of
Human Services**
Division of Child Support Enforcement
750 North State Street
Jackson, MS 39205
800-345-6349
www.mdhs.state.ms.us

MISSOURI
Department of Social Services
Division of Child Support
Enforcement
800-859-7999
www.dss.state.mo.us

MONTANA
**Department of Public Health
and Human Services**
Child Support Enforcement
P.O. Box 202943
Helena, MT 59620-2943
406-444-9855
Fax: 406-444-1370
www.dphhs.mt.gov

NEBRASKA
Health and Human Services
Child Support Enforcement
P.O. Box 94728
Lincoln, NE 68509-4728
877-631-9973
402-441-8715
www.hhs.state.ne.us/cse

NEVADA
Department of Human Resources
Welfare Division—Child Support
Enforcement
1470 East College Parkway
Carson City, NV 89706
775-684-0500
www.welfare.state.nv.us/child.htm

NEW HAMPSHIRE
Department of Health and Human Services
NH DHHS Division of
Child Support Service
129 Pleasant Street
Concord, NH 03301-3857
800-852-3345
www.dhhs.state.nh.us

NEW JERSEY
Department of Human Services
Child Support Hotline: 877-655-4371
www.njchildsupport.org

NEW MEXICO
Child Support Enforcement Division
P.O. Box 25110
Santa Fe, NM 87504
Within NM: 800-288-7207
Outside NM: 800-585-7631
http://childsupport.hsd.state.nm.us

NEW YORK
New York State Office of Temporary and Disability Assistance
40 North Pearl Street
Albany, NY 12243
800-846-0773
www.otda.state.ny.us

NORTH CAROLINA
Department of Health and Human Services
2201 Mail Service Center
Raleigh, NC 27699-2201
800-992-9457
www.dhhs.state.nc.us

NORTH DAKOTA
Department of Human Services
Child Support Enforcement Division
1600 East Century Avenue
P.O. Box 7190
Bismark, ND 58507-7190
800-366-6888
www.childsupportnd.com

OHIO
Office of Child Support
Ohio Department of Job and
Family Services
30 East Broad Street
32nd Floor
Columbus, Ohio 43215-3414
614-752-6561
Fax: 614-752-9760
http://jfs.ohio.gov/OCS

OKLAHOMA
Department of Human Services
P.O. Box 25352
Oklahoma City, OK 73152
KIDS LINE: 800-522-2922
www.okdhs.org

OREGON
Oregon Department of Human Services
500 Summer Street, N.E.
Salem, OR 97301
503-945-5944
Fax: 503-378-2897
www.oregon.gov/DHS

PENNSYLVANIA
Department of Public Welfare
Health and Welfare Building
P.O. Box 2675
Harrisburg, PA17105-2675
Child Support Helpline: 800-932-0211
www.dpw.state.pa.us

RHODE ISLAND
Department of Administration
Division of Taxation—
Child Support Enforcement
77 Dorrance Street
Providence, RI 02930
401-222-3845
www.childsupportliens.com

SOUTH CAROLINA
Department of Social Services—
Child Support Enforcement
P.O. Box 1520
Columbia, SC 29202-1520
800-768-5858
www.state.sc.us/dss

SOUTH DAKOTA
Department of Social Services
Division of Child Support
Enforcement
700 Governors Drive
Pierre, SD 57501
800-286-9145
www.state.sd.us

TENNESSEE
Department of Human Services
400 Deaderick Street
15th Floor
Nashville, TN 37248-0001
615-313-4700
http://tennessee.gov/humanserv

TEXAS
Office of Attorney General
P.O. Box 12548
Austin, TX 78711-2548
800-252-8014
512-460-6000
www.oag.state.tx.us

UTAH
Department of Human Services
Office of Recovery Services
515 East 100 South
P.O. Box 45033
Salt Lake City, UT 84102
800-662-8525
www.ors.state.ut.us

VERMONT
Office of Child Support
Vermont Agency of Human Services
103 South Main Street
Waterbury, VT 05671-1901
800-786-3214
www.ocs.state.vt.us

VIRGINIA
Department of Social Services
Child Support Enforcement
7 North Eighth Street
Richmond, VA 23219
804-726-7000
www.dss.state.va.us

WASHINGTON
Department of Social and Health
Services
Division of Child Support
P.O. Box 9162
Olympia, WA 98507-9162
800-457-6202
www.wa.gov

WEST VIRGINIA
Department of Health and
Human Services
Bureau for Child Support
Enforcement
800-249-3778
www.wvdhhr.org

WISCONSIN
Wisconsin Department of
Workforce Development
Child Support Program
201 East Washington Avenue
Madison, WI 53702
608-267-4337
www.dwd.state.wi.us

WYOMING
Child Support Enforcement
2020 Carey Avenue
Suite 601
Cheyenne, WY 82001
307-635-3365
http://wyoming.gov

INDEX

ABOUT THE AUTHOR

Jacqueline D. Stanley received her law degree from Wake Forest University. Ms. Stanley has coauthored many self-help legal guides, including *How to File for Divorce in North Carolina*. She currently resides in Greensboro, North Carolina.